Interviews
That Get
Results
Suzee Vlk

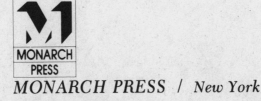

MONARCH PRESS / *New York*

Published by MONARCH PRESS
A Division of Simon & Schuster, Inc.
Simon & Schuster Building
1230 Avenue of the Americas
New York, New York 10020

MONARCH PRESS and colophon are registered trademarks
of Simon & Schuster, Inc.

Designed by Irving Perkins Associates
Manufactured in the United States of America
10 9 8 7 6 5 4 3 2 1

Library of Congress Catalog Card Number: 83-63395

ISBN: 0-671-50457-6

Contents

After

Appendices

Introduction

THE PURPOSE OF an interview is to get results. The result may be that you are hired for that particular position you interviewed for. The result may be that you are hired for a different position. The result may be that you are not hired but are kept in mind for future openings. The result may be that you are not hired by the firm with which you interviewed, but are recommended to another firm, which then offers you a position. Each result was affected by your interview. The interview is definitely a critical step in your job-seeking process.

Interviewing is a skill. It is not a talent, like musical or artistic abilities. It is a learned set of rules and suggestions that *anyone* can master with a little work. Whether you are self-confident and assured, or timid and retiring, you can learn how to promote your best points and deemphasize your weaknesses. Whether you have a great deal of education and experience, or are just entering the job market, you can learn how to make the interviewer think that your background is perfect.

This book is for everyone who realizes the importance of a good interview. You have probably spent years in education or in the job market learning skills. Why not spend some time learning how to sell yourself sufficiently well to be able to utilize those skills in the position of your choice?

This book is divided into three units. The first unit is called *Before* and tells you what to do before the interview. Much of the success of an interview depends on how well prepared, how confident you are before entering the interviewer's office. The second unit is called *During*. This unit tells you how to conduct yourself during the interview, and covers such topics as handling the questions you are asked, asking questions of your own, and observing the facilities. The final unit is called *After*. It tells you how to deal with offers or rejections in the most professional manner possible. Sample letters are included that you may want to use (individualized to your own situations) for guidance.

Read the whole book before going to the interview. Select the sections that are the most relevant to your personal needs and review them carefully. Remember, the more you know and the more you are prepared for before going into the interview, the more confident and professional you will seem to the interviewer.

Good interviews get positive results. By studying this book, you will be assuring yourself that you have done your best to get the result that you most want. Good luck!

Before

PREPARATION IS THE key. *Before* going to the interview, you should do certain activities, study certain subjects or persons, assemble certain materials. If you are prepared, you will feel more confident, more assured, more relaxed. Such an attitude cannot help but impress the interviewer, who has probably seen many nervous, unprepared applicants before you. Your preparation will also show the interviewer how seriously you take the interview, and how professional you are to have done background research.

The following materials show you what steps need to be taken *before* you go to the interview. You will learn what research needs to be done, what documentation needs to be gathered together, what questions need to be formulated. You will also be given suggestions on grooming and dress.

Study this unit carefully. Remember that once you are at the interview, nothing is more profitless and futile than thinking about all those things you should have done before. A little time spent on the activities suggested in this unit will help you be prepared, confident... professional.

DOING YOUR HOMEWORK

1. RESEARCHING THE COMPANY
2. RESEARCHING THE INTERVIEWER
3. RESEARCHING YOUR FELLOW WORKERS
4. REFERENCE MATERIALS AND SOURCES
5. MISCELLANEOUS

Before you go to your interview, you should be fully prepared. You will want to know everything possible about your prospective company, interviewer, and fellow workers. The following materials

5

will help acquaint you with the considerations you should research and the places you may find your information.

Researching the Company

Remember that you want to learn about the company as much as it wants to learn about you. There is no reason that you should not "interview" the firm before you are interviewed yourself. Try to find out as much of the following information as you can about your prospective employer.

Learn when the firm was established, by whom, and for what reason. You should learn who has merged with this firm, or who controls it as a partner or subsidiary. Such knowledge will impress the interviewer with your determination to be a loyal and knowledgeable worker. The ultimate goal of gaining this information, though, is not to impress the interviewer with how much you know, but to get an idea of where the company has been and where it is heading.

Learn about the goals of the firm. If you are going to be a part of the business, you certainly should try to learn what the firm sees in its future. You may find that the business wants to expand or diversify, or merely to sell out after making a profit. If the goals of the firm provide you with an opportunity to meet your own personal goals, you will know that you are searching in the right place. Also, when the interviewer asks you for your goals, you will be able to give him or her those which are also the goals of the company. The interviewer then feels you are the proper person for the job, as your future and that of the firm meld so well.

Obtain information about the financial status of the firm. If the firm is experiencing failures in the product line, or is not meeting its obligations on time, you know that you may not have much of a future with such a company. If you are interviewing for a job as a commissioned sales rep., for instance, you should try to find out whether the company has a reputation for promptly delivering products ordered, for this will have a direct effect on your ability to keep your customers and earn money. If the company is in bad financial trouble, you may be back on the street looking for another job in a year's time. However, if the company has done well recently and has a solid financial base, you know that your job probably would be secure. If you are in the type of position where your finances are tied to the success of the firm (as with a profit-sharing plan), knowledge of the financial situation is especially critical.

Find out what the employee turnover rate is. This information may be obtained from two primary sources. Most employment agencies have sent many job seekers to particular firms and probably have a good overall idea of the employee turnover rate. Also, corporate published materials, such as in-house newsletters or status reports frequently give the turnover rate if it is significantly lower than those of other firms in the same industry.

If the employees in the firm leave after six months, you may assume that there are problems with morale or labor relations. Of course, in some fields, it is customary to have a quick turnover (such as in manual labor or domestic services). If the employees have all been with the firm for years, you may feel more secure in joining the organization.

Researching the Interviewer

You should be able to learn exactly who will be interviewing you. If your first interview is going to be with the personnel director, you will probably be told this by whoever sets up the interview. You can ask the personnel director who will be interviewing you next: the person you will be working for? his or her assistant? Take the time to learn a little about the person with whom you will be speaking. This is not so that you can unctuously flatter the interviewer; it is so that you will be able to know that you are prepared and thus feel more comfortable.

Try to learn about the interviewer's status in the firm. The interviewer may be only a clerk, an hourly worker who merely fills in the forms. Or you may be interviewed by the head of personnel, who will have a major voice in deciding whether or not you are hired. You may not want to reveal certain aspects of your background to the people in personnel since they feel an obligation to screen out unqualified applicants, and you may not get a chance to explain how your background really *does* apply. But remember to make a good impression on everyone you meet: a negative comment about you from a secretary could very well destroy your chances for the job.

Researching Your Fellow Workers

You should try to find out as much as possible about those with whom you will be working. This is especially true if you are going to be an integral part of a team project. Learning the accomplishments, education and training, and background of your boss, peers, and subordinates will make you more confident in your dealings with them. Make an effort to obtain information on the following topics.

The significant contributions the people have made to the firm or the industry. If you know of an accomplishment, you may gain respect for the person and have a greater desire to work with him or her. You may mention your knowledge of the accomplishment to the interviewer, confident that such praise will eventually go back to its recipient.

The training and education the people have. Such information allows you to determine whether you will fit in well, will have to work to obtain more knowledge, or will be better trained than the others. Depending on your position and your personal proclivities, you may want to work with those from whom you feel you could learn, or those whom you feel you could teach.

Reference Materials and Sources

The following material gives suggestions on where to obtain the information discussed in the preceding sections.

"HEADHUNTERS"

"Headhunters" are the employment agency workers, the counselors and job-finders. Most good "headhunters" know about the company and the people within it and are your best source of information. Remember that you are probably not the first worker the counselor has sent to the company; he or she has received feedback, either negative or positive, which can be passed on to you.

NEWSPAPERS

Both the local newspaper and the in-house newspaper (a short newsletter published by the company itself and distributed to its employees) will have information on the company. Such sources may tell you of personnel changes, special contracts awarded, or even criminal charges filed. A library or the offices of the local newspaper will have back copies you can look through.

Large newspapers, published in major cities and distributed nationally (such as *The New York Times* or *The Los Angeles Times*), are also significant sources of information. If you are researching a large corporation that is national or multinational in its business dealings, you may consult general business papers such as *The Wall Street Journal* as well.

"WHO'S WHO"

For every major industry, there are books called the "Who's Who" series. Such books will give the name of the person, and relevant information such as education, accomplishments, clubs and organizations, and special qualifications or honors. Such books are invaluable to you for researching a prospective employer. These books are available at most libraries.

OTHER PERSONS

Naturally you will want to talk to former and current employees of the firm if at all possible. Just remember that the information you are receiving from them reflects their own opinions and may or may not be factual. Most persons color their comments according to their personal bias. Try to verify any information you receive.

INDUSTRY DIRECTORIES

Most libraries have several industry directories available in the reference department. The reference librarian can quickly tell you what sources are the standard in your industry. Some examples are *Literary Market Place*, *The Red Book*, *Martindale-Hubble* and *Standard and Poor's* publications.

FINANCIAL STATEMENTS

Publicly owned corporations are required to publish yearly financial reports in which they give information on assets and debits. Such statements may help you understand the overall structure of a firm and its degree of stability. They may be requested from the company itself or found in large libraries.

TRADE MAGAZINES

Virtually every industry has several trade publications. Examples of these publications are *Advertising Age* and *Computer News*. Public libraries often have back issues of these magazines on microfilm so that you can quickly find specific articles relating to your company.

Miscellaneous

There are other projects you should consider as part of your homework. Some are discussed in greater detail in later chapters; however, take a moment to note the following.

A. MARKET SALARY SURVEYS

Before you go into an interview during which you may be offered a salary, make certain that you have surveyed the industry to find the average salary for one in your position. Most major industries publish salary reports that are available at public libraries. Ask the reference librarian for help.

B. DOCUMENTATION

There are many documents you will want to assemble and have ready for the interview. The next section covers these papers more thoroughly. Be aware that assembling the documentation may take weeks or months (for example, if you send for college transcripts); you are wise to begin preparing early.

C. LEGAL RIGHTS

Learn your rights before you go to an interview. You should know what questions the interviewer may and may not ask (for example, in many instances the interviewer may *not* ask whether you are married or single, or whether you are pregnant, or whether you have had a serious illness such as cancer). You should prepare to deal with such questions either by bypassing them diplomatically, answering them, or refusing to answer them. You should know whether you will be able to change your mind within a certain set period of time after you sign a contract. You should know the laws against discrimination based on race or gender or religion or a handicap. For information, you may call the local chapter of the ACLU (American Civil Liberties Union); you probably will be sent a short pamphlet outlining your rights.

Doing your homework is at least as important as going to the interview. If your homework has been prepared and you are confident, your attitude will be one of professional self-assurance. The following checklist will help you make certain that you have done the work you should have prior to going for the interview.

CHECKLIST

1. Do I know the history and the goals of the firm?
2. Do I know the financial status of the firm?
3. Do I know the employee turnover rate of the firm?
4. Do I know who will be interviewing me?
5. Do I know the interviewer's position within the firm?

6. Do I know the background, accomplishments, and skills of the other employees?
7. Have I asked the "headhunters," as well as past and present employees, for information about the firm?
8. Have I checked newspapers, trade directories and other sources for information about the firm and my boss?
9. Have I done a salary survey and prepared all the necessary documentation?
10. Am I aware of my legal rights?

ASSEMBLING YOUR DOCUMENTATION

1. RESUMES AND REFERENCES
2. DIPLOMAS, LICENSES, AND TRANSCRIPTS
3. PAST EMPLOYMENT DOCUMENTS
4. PUBLISHED MATERIALS
5. MISCELLANEOUS

When you interview, you want to present yourself as a well-organized, prepared person. Part of being prepared is to assemble and bring with you all the documentation the interviewer might ask for. A review of the following materials will help you determine which documents you should collect and take to the interview.

Resumes and References

Even if you have sent your resume and letters of recommendation or reference in to the company prior to obtaining the interview, take duplicates with you. Especially in large companies, the person with whom you will be speaking may not have those materials on hand.

Bring up-to-date, complete, professional resumes and references. If some time has elapsed since you sent your original resume and reference in to the company, and you have since added material to those documents, make certain that the new information is included. If you have included no new material, check to be sure that the resume you are bringing is the same one that you have sent in to the company before (so that you and the interviewer are speaking about the same document). A sample resume is included at the end of this unit.

Be certain that your letters of reference are topical and related to the position for which you are applying. A common error applicants make is trying to force extraneous material on the interviewer. Unless it is absolutely relevant to the job you are seeking, do not give the interviewer letters from your family minister or rabbi, or glowing paeans from your high school principal. Remember that the only question the interviewer really is concerned with is, "Is this the best person for the job?"

Bring at least two copies of everything. If the interviewer doesn't want something, you can keep it in your briefcase; if the documents are accepted, you will appear well-prepared and courteous by having a copy for the interviewer and one that can be passed along to your prospective superior.

Diplomas, Licenses, and Transcripts

If the position requires that you have a specific degree or license or certificate, you may need to furnish proof that you possess one. In most cases, it is best not to volunteer a diploma or certificate unless it is asked for. But be prepared just in case. Never give an original to the interviewer. There is always the possibility that it will be lost. Keep the originals at home and bring in two copies to be left permanently with the firm.

As with references and resumes, make certain that the materials you are introducing are relevant to your job performance. Even though you may be very proud of your special Ham operator's license, it probably is not going to impress someone who is interviewing you for a position as a chef.

If you do not have a degree, but have taken specific classes and done well in them, you might want to bring a copy of your transcript with you. This is especially true if you have gone to an excellent school, received good grades, or taken difficult subjects.

Past Employment Documents

You may want to furnish materials from previous jobs. Of course, you will be selective, choosing only those materials that are complimentary to you, that are relevant to the position you are seeking, and that are relatively recent. Include the following materials if they are relevant to you.

Salary history and merit review papers. If you are proud of the salary you have earned previously, or if your salary has increased steadily over the years, showing that the company appreciated your work, take such a record with you, if your company will release it. If your previous firm gave merit reviews and yours had comments that were positive, include those in your portfolio as well. But be careful that if you bring one set of documents, you have no gaps in them. In other words, you do not want to bring your merit reviews for three out of five years; that merely calls the interviewer's attention to those two missing years. He or she will naturally wonder what was wrong during that time, why you don't want him or her to see those documents.

Customer praise letters or thank you's. If you are going into a job that requires you deal with the public, any letters you have received from previously satisfied customers will be impressive. Choose a few of the most complimentary letters, being certain that they stress those characteristics that this interviewer is most interested in (such as professionalism, patience, courtesy with a difficult customer, and thoroughness). If you are not going to be dealing on a one-to-one basis with the public, you may still want to include any thank-you letters that your firm received on a project on which you worked. For example, a firm might have written to thank your company for bringing in a project on time and under budget.

Proof of any special awards or honors received from previous employers. You might have been named the employee of the week, or might have gotten a special bonus for an appropriate suggestion you supplied. Bring proof of such an award, be it a letter from your firm or a notice in the company newsletter. Remember that you want to show the interviewer that you have done more than just the basic job.

Published Materials

You might have written blueprints, job descriptions, reports, or other projects that were published in trade journals or special papers. Bring anything that has been put into print and circulated.

Bring two copies of all published materials, showing when and where they were published. It does little good to bring in a copy of a report and tell the interviewer it was published. Bring in a copy of the magazine in which it was published, showing the date. If your publication was a training manual or something used solely in-house, (that is, within the company itself), bring a copy of that.

Also bring any follow-up correspondence from published materials. If an article of yours was published, you probably received letters from others in your field, praising your work or asking for more details. Choose two or three letters that are from respected members of your profession to show to the interviewer. This will show him or her that you are known in your field and your work is familiar to others.

Miscellaneous

Bring business cards. Even if you are unemployed and have no "business" card per se, it is a good idea to have some sort of card printed with your name, degrees, telephone number and address on it. Many businesspeople find that keeping cards is easier than keeping a large address file. A card is quick and easy to refer to. Bring a few in case you talk to more than one person.

Bring a list of the questions you want to ask. No matter how carefully you rehearse the interview at home, there may come a moment during the conversation when you forget what you wanted to ask. A simple list of topics that you want to cover or questions you want to ask will be invaluable at such a moment. Often interviewers are impressed at the organization the applicant shows by having prepared such a list.

Planning and preparation help you be self-confident and help you impress the interviewer. Having all your documentation assembled allows you to give the interviewer whatever he or she asks for. Before you leave for the interview, take a look at the following checklist and make certain that you have all the relevant information.

CHECKLIST

1. Do I have an up-to-date, professional-looking resume?
2. Do I have letters of reference or recommendations?
3. Do I have proof of my diplomas, certificates, or licenses?
4. Do I want to take information on my salary history and merit reviews?
5. Do I have letters of thanks or praise from customers?
6. Do I have proof of special awards or honors?
7. Do I have copies of published materials or articles about me?
8. Do I have my research materials on the company, my prospective employers, and the interviewer?
9. Do I have cards with my name, degrees, telephone number, and address?
10. Are all my materials copies (not originals) of relevant information?

DETERMINING GOALS

1. JOB DUTIES AND RESPONSIBILITIES
2. JOB TITLE AND STATUS
3. JOB FUTURE
4. SALARY VERSUS "PERKS"
5. TIME AND HOLIDAYS
6. WORKING CONDITIONS

Ideally, you should assess your career goals in the first stage of the job-hunting process, well ahead of the interview. But if you have

• *Sample Resume*

George Marcy
1234 Miami Drive
Jessica, Maryland 20817
(619) 555-1212

Education

MASTER OF ELECTRICAL ENGINEERING, 1980
California State Polytechnic University
San Luis Obispo, California

BACHELOR OF COMPUTER SCIENCE, 1977
California State Polytechnic University
San Luis Obispo, California

Work Experience

1980-1983   SENIOR SYSTEMS ANALYST
             Ewing Computer Corporation
             Washington, D.C.

1977-1980   GRADUATE TEACHING ASSISTANT
             Computer Science/Electrical Engineering classes
             California State Polytechnic University
             San Luis Obispo, California

1975-1977   PROGRAMMER
             Baranko Enterprises, Inc.
             San Luis Obispo, California

Hardware Experience

IBM 370/168	IBM 370/178	IBM 3033
PDP-11 LSI	IMSAI	BURROUGHS 7800

Operating Systems

CP/M	APPLE DOS	MP/M
USCD-P	VAX/VMS	C/CS

Programming Languages

COBOL	UCSD PASCAL	FORTRAN IV
BASIC	BAL	FORTRAN 77

References

Professional references are available upon request.

gotten an interview before you have had a chance to formulate your ideas on this subject, prepare your personal and professional goals now—*before* the interview. You should think about the various aspects of your working life so that you are able to ask intelligent questions that will enable you to determine whether this particular job is the best one for you. The following material will help you determine your goals.

Job Duties and Responsibilities

What do you want to do as part of your job? Perhaps, more importantly, what do you *not* want to do as part of your job? ("I don't do windows!") To determine what you want from the position, carefully consider the following topics.

Specific daily tasks. Depending on the job, your daily tasks may be routine or may vary nearly every day. You should be aware of what you will be called upon to do. Whether you are the type of person who dislikes routine, or the type of person who likes the comfort of doing the same activities regularly, you will want to work at a job that satisfies you.

Schedules and time pressures. Some people work well under pressure; others become flustered and unable to perform. Determine whether you are the type of person who wants to know exact dates by which a project must be done, or whether you are willing to work in a more fluid situation.

Responsibility over other workers. You may not like to give orders to others. Think about whether you would enjoy or even tolerate having others working for you, depending on you for guidance and authority. The position you choose should be one that allows you to give or execute orders, according to your personality.

Job Title and Status

For some people, the proper professional title ("Senior Vice President," "Executive Administrative Assistant") is at least as important as the salary or the "perks." Consider the following topics to determine how critical status is to your professional life.

An impressive professional title. If you use your title or position when calling and introducing yourself to people, or when sending letters out, chances are you find it very significant and important. If you answer the question, "What do you do?" with your job title ("I'm the Senior Vice President...") rather than with a description of your duties, you know that the title is vital to your personal satisfaction. In such a case, you might want to be certain that you would be given an impressive title in your new job.

The position within the firm's hierarchy. You might be very irritated to have an office without a window, or not to have a reserved parking space. In that case, you probably would also be irritated by having a job title that is less impressive than those of your fellow workers. While others may not care whether you are the "Senior" worker or not, you might find it is worth discussing this point during the interview.

Job Future

The future that a job holds is very significant to many people. Ostensibly, you are going through the entire interview process to better your position, so that your future will be more pleasant and comfortable. Consider the following.

Estimated length of time at this firm or in this position. You may only be taking the job to make a little money to live on while you are going to school or while you are looking for a better position or for a new line of work. If such is the case, then job security and a golden future are not your major considerations. You may be more interested in taking a high salary from the beginning and giving up any chance of future profit-sharing or promotions.

Your goals in one year/five years/ten years. This is a point frequently raised by interviewers. You should definitely have thought about such goals prior to going for the interview. Think of your goals from all levels: financial, professional, personal. Make certain that you have at least a vague idea of what you would like to be doing, what responsibilities or status you would like to have, and where you would like to be working.

Your goals and views regarding retirement. Depending on your age, you might not even think about retirement. However, especially if you are interviewing for a position at which you intend to spend many years, you should definitely consider this topic. Determine whether you would like to retire early and perhaps get another job (as persons who worked in the military or for the government often do) or whether you would like to stay at your position as long as you are capable of doing so. If you plan to retire as quickly as possible, you should look into the retirement plans of the various firms with which you are interviewing.

Salary Versus "Perks"

"Perks" are perquisites, those little extra benefits that make a job more appealing. Typical perks are the use of the company car, or having an expense account. Give some thought to whether you want a large paycheck every week, or whether you would take less money given the proper extras. Think also about the following.

The importance of the cash. If you have many obligations, such as repaying student loans or meeting mortgage payments, you probably want to have the largest paycheck you can find. You might not care about having free seats at the local football stadium.

The importance of the perks. More and more companies are implementing dental and medical plans. If you have a large family, the savings on dental and medical bills can be significant. Before you go to the interview, take the time to review the medical expenses your family has incurred annually; you might be willing to accept a lesser salary given better medical benefits.

The future value of the perks. Some firms allow their workers to continue their education while being employed. Obviously, a better education will influence your whole future. In particular, many firms have connections with prestigious colleges and universities, allowing you to get a degree from a school that might not otherwise accept you. In such an instance, taking a lesser salary in favor of the perk would be an investment in yourself.

Time and Holidays

You may find that you cannot work a forty-hour week; you may want to work fewer hours at a more intensive rate, or more hours at a more leisurely rate. You may find that you need to take many holidays, to prevent "burnout" or to satisfy family obligations. When considering your goals relating to working time and holidays, think of the following matters.

Regular hours as opposed to a more flexible schedule. Some people prefer to go to work at the same time every day, to get into a routine where home and work are separated completely. Such people leave their professional considerations behind them at the end of the day. Others like to do work at home, and dislike having to punch a time clock or go to an office at the same time, day after day. Determine which type of person you are, and find out from the interviewer whether you would have any latitude in your working hours and locations.

Overtime. Normally, employers don't "expect" overtime; it somehow seems to arise when a project is behind schedule and you are the one responsible for its timely completion. If you know that you would not be willing to work long hours occasionally to make certain that a project is completed on time, you might consider not accepting a position where time is of the essence. Whether you will be paid for overtime or have "exempt" status may also affect your decision to accept a position.

Personal obligations on holidays. You may have family obligations that require you not work on holidays. You may have religious convictions that make you insist on taking certain days or dates off. Many firms publish a list of "accepted" holidays. Others allow you to determine which holidays you want. Since the interviewer is quite apt to ask you about your holiday preferences, be certain that you have taken a calendar and looked over the dates prior to the interview. Determine exactly what dates you must have off, and which ones you are flexible on.

Working Conditions

You will probably be in the office eight hours a day. The conditions in which you work should be as important to you as the conditions in your own home. To make certain that you have thought about the conditions in which you will spend your days, carefully review the following concepts.

Personal physical needs. Allergies may force you to work only in well-ventilated, air-conditioned, non-smoking offices. Poor vision may require you to be certain that lighting is especially brilliant. A propensity towards migraines might mean that you will want to work in a very quiet building. Take the time to think about what aspects of an office are important to you.

Impossible working conditions. While most job applicants try to be flexible and give the impression that they are willing to work most anywhere, you must realize that taking a job where the physical conditions are unpleasant only means that you will soon quit and have to go through this entire interviewing process again. Check your "pet irritations" to see whether they are worth mentioning. Some persons cannot work in a building where the P.A. system constantly plays music as a "soothing" background. Others will not work in a location near children, as the incessant noise irritates them.

Before going to the interview, determine your personal goals and objectives. Take the time to think about what you want from a job, what you need from a job, what you demand from a job. Of course, you are not going to go into the interview making dogmatic statements of what you will and will not accept; there is no surer way to alienate an interviewer and make certain you are not offered the position. However, knowing in your own mind what is or is not acceptable to you will allow you to make a more intelligent decision on the position should it be offered to you. The following checklist will help you choose the topics that are important to you.

CHECKLIST

1. What will be my daily tasks?
2. Will I be working under pressure to meet a deadline?
3. Will I be responsible for the work of others?
4. How important are my job title and status to me?
5. How long do I want to remain at this position or in this firm?
6. What are my short- and long-range professional goals?
7. Do I want cash more than I want special perks?
8. What value do the perks have to me and my family and to our future?
9. Do I want a flexible schedule or do I need regular hours and mandatory holidays?
10. What special physical conditions am I looking for in the firm?

GROOMING AND DRESS

1. VARIABLES
2. CLOTHING
3. SCENT

4. COSMETICS
5. HAIR
6. ACCESSORIES
7. PREPARATION

Although the statements have become clichés, most of us would probably agree that "Clothes make the man" and "First impressions are important." When you walk into an office for an interview, your appearance is the first thing the interviewer notices about you. He or she will retain that image even after you have begun talking and gotten to know one another. Later, when asked to describe the new applicant, the interviewer will most likely not state, "She knows BASIC and COBOL languages" but rather, "She is tall and has carrot red hair she wears in frizzy curls." Physical descriptions often are given before and remembered longer than qualifications, regardless of how impressive those qualifications are. Therefore, it is critical that you give much thought and attention to your grooming and dress prior to an interview.

Variables

At each step prior to your interview, you must set goals for yourself. The matter of grooming and dress is no exception; you must determine your objectives prior to choosing your clothing.

The way you should dress depends to some extent on the company to which you are applying. If you are going to work in a law firm, you know that the atmosphere will be rather formal, requiring that you always wear a suit or dress. If you are going to work in a computer firm where the atmosphere is more casual, you might find that wearing slacks and a nice shirt is sufficient. If you are going to work as a plumber, you certainly do not want to be so formally dressed that you give the impression that you are above getting yourself dirty. In short, suit your appearance to the level found within the rest of the corporation.

Likewise, your dress will vary depending on the specific position for which you are applying. If you are applying for an executive position, dress like an executive. You might have to bankrupt yourself temporarily, but buy good quality clothing. If you interview in a $49.95 suit or a $9.99 dress, you probably will not be considered prime executive material. If your financial situation is such that you honestly cannot afford to buy truly good quality clothing, purchase just one good piece (for example, a silk tie or a silk scarf) and make that piece the focal point of your outfit.

If you are not interviewing to become an executive, determine the position you want and dress accordingly. You might even want to watch the people who currently hold the positions you want (for example, when the building empties at closing time, you could be seated in your car in the parking lot and watch the workers exit, noting the clothing styles) to make certain that you fit the image the interviewer has of a worker in your desired position. Basically, you should dress according to the job you are seeking.

You should dress in a manner appropriate to your age. If you are young, you want to dress like a young professional. If you are more mature, you do *not* want to make the mistake of trying to dress in fashions for the very young. While you may think that you look quite stylish, others will probably view you as somewhat foolish. Dress your age.

Clothing

Clothing may be the single most important feature of your appearance. As you choose the clothing for your interview, consider the following.

Wear clothing that flatters you. No matter how carefully you research the firm and choose clothing to meet your objectives, if you do not wear clothing that flatters you, you will not look good. There is no sense in looking "proper" if you don't look neat and attractive.

Make sure your clothing is in excellent condition. Of course, you will have dry-cleaned or washed and pressed whatever you are going to wear. But take the time to check the little points. Are any threads hanging? Are there wrinkles in the back of your clothing that you can't see by a cursory glance in the mirror? Are there runs in your nylons? Are the heels of your shoes worn down? When you sit and talk to the interviewer for a length of time, he or she will have the opportunity to look at you carefully and add up all those little things that add to or detract from your appearance.

Wear clothing in which you are comfortable. Too many people go and purchase new clothing for the interview, then wear it for the first time during the meeting. They are uncomfortable in clothing that has not been broken in. This means that they sit and fidget, surreptitiously loosening waistlines or shuffling out of too-tight shoes. Be certain that you have worn your new clothes at least once before.

Scent

If the interviewer can smell you before he or she sees you, you probably are making a bad impression before you walk into the room. While humans do not have the well-developed sense of scent that other animals possess, we do note odors, sometimes subconsciously. Most important is that you don't wear too *much* perfume. Everyone has probably had the experience of being trapped on a bus or airplane with someone who seems to have bathed in scent. No matter how nice the smell is, too much is not pleasant. If you can still smell the scent strongly ten minutes after you have put it on, you are probably wearing too much. Remember that you and the interviewer will be together in a small office for some time. Be considerate.

Be sure you smell nice. Use mouthwash or breath mints if necessary. Of course you will have cleaned yourself thoroughly before leaving home, but occasionally after a long ride to the interview, you will find that you need a refresher. Many stores sell small freshening towels (something like the wet napkins people use on picnics, after eating chicken) that can be used to wipe yourself off quickly. Special deodorant talcum powders are available to neutralize skin bacteria for hours, preventing any odor. Please remember that cologne is not meant to cover up odors. Wearing cologne on top of an unclean body does very little good.

Wear an appropriate scent. There is one type of cologne that is appropriate for evenings and one that is appropriate for days (this applies to men's colognes too). Try to wear a light, fresh cologne (usually something with a lemon or other fruit scent) rather than a heavy, cloying perfume.

Cosmetics

Men as well as women should be aware that there are cosmetics that are appropriate to use. Of course, women are more familiar with make-up than are men, but both genders should follow these suggestions.

Don't wear too much make-up. If you are wearing pancake make-up, red rouge, and heavy lipstick, you probably will not look appropriate. Again, this depends on what type of job you are applying for. However, the general rule is that "less is more." Look at yourself in the mirror—then wipe off about half of what you are wearing. Remember that often you will be interviewed by a man who doesn't like overly made-up women, or by a woman who herself is a professional and knows how to dress and make up appropriately.

Don't wear too little make-up. You might want to enhance your appearance. Many people wear a small amount of "bronzer," a cosmetic that adds a healthy glow to the face. If your skin is naturally sallow or light, choose a foundation that gives you some color. You do not want to give an anemic, washed-out appearance. Nearly everyone responds favorably to a person who appears ruddy and healthy.

Check to make certain the make-up is correctly applied. Many people apply cosmetics in the light of their bathroom mirror. Then during the interview, another type of lighting is used and the make-up that looked perfect at home could, for example, assume a greenish tint that looks terrible. If at all possible, make up in the same type of lighting that the offices have. Check very carefully to make certain that your cosmetics have not smeared (black lines under the eyes from mascara are especially irritating) and that you have gotten no make-up on your clothing.

Hair

Hair is sometimes called the "crowning glory." It certainly is one of the most noticeable features of anyone's appearance. Review the following suggestions about your hair.

Keep your hair clean and natural. Make certain that your hair has been freshly washed and has no trace of oil or dirt. It should be shiny, fresh-smelling, and pleasant to see. It should also be natural. This means that you do not want to put on a huge amount of hair spray to hold it in what you think is the perfect style. Try to wear it as close to the way you will always be wearing it as possible. During the interview, you do not want to be awkward, holding your head as if you were afraid that your hair would be mussed.

Wear an appropriate style. If you are going to be a professional, you should look like a professional. For men, extremely long hair or outrageous styles (such as a Mohawk haircut) are definitely deleterious to your chances of being hired. A neat, well-cut, and styled hairdo that flatters your features is important. As before, you want to consider the attitudes and prejudices of your interviewer. If you are being interviewed by someone older than you, you should probably have your hair relatively short. If you are being interviewed by a younger person, you might be able to wear a longer style.

Give consideration to wearing a beard or a moustache. Your decision really depends on whether you are comfortable wearing facial hair and whether it looks good on you, but you also must consider the nature of your position. If you know that you will be representing the firm to conservative customers, you probably should be clean shaven. If you know that many others in that firm wear facial hair, you could feel comfortable wearing it yourself. However, the best rule is that when in doubt, shave it off. You can always regrow it when you feel more secure in your position.

Basically the same rules for hairstyles apply to women. Forgo any outrageous hairstyles, or styles that are truly out of fashion (such as teased bee-hive hairdos). If you are applying for a job in a high-fashion industry, you may be able to wear a less conservative style; in any case, try to wear something you will not have to comb and style every ten minutes.

Accessories

You learned earlier that if you cannot afford a good quality wardrobe, you should invest in at least one good accessory. Often, the accessories make or break the outfit. If you are called back for more than one interview, you may wear the same suit or dress again (since you wore your best quality one to the first interview); in such an instance, choosing the appropriate accessories can make the outfit seem new.

Choose the appropriate style and amount of jewelry. There is no need (unless you are going to work in a high-fashion job) to wear an excessive amount of jewelry. If you have one particular piece of which you are proud, you might want to emphasize it. Remember to choose a piece that is appropriate to the image you are presenting. If you want to be an executive, you do not wear a Mickey Mouse pin, regardless of how many diamonds it has on it. Most importantly, do not wear jewelry that makes a noise or distracts from the interview. Necklaces that dangle and spin, or bangle bracelets that always shift and make noise can be very irritating. Keep it simple.

Carry a briefcase. Unless you are applying for a manual laborer's job, carry some type of briefcase or attache case with you. It makes no difference that you may have nothing in it but your lunch and bus fare—carry one. Even if you never take it to work again, carry it to the interview. A briefcase gives you more authority and can be a very confidence-inspiring prop. Again, be certain that it is the best quality one that you can afford. You might want to borrow one from a friend just for the interview.

Preparation

The night before the interview, have all your clothing and accessories laid out, cleaned, pressed, and ready to go. Make certain that you have tried on everything, gotten an objective opinion from a friend or relative, and spent some time in the clothing to make certain it is comfortable. On the day of the interview, you want to be able simply to put on your clothes and go, free of all worries or decision-making.

The way you look, smell, and present yourself is critical to any interview. Many factors of the interview are somewhat beyond your control, but grooming and dress are matters of which you have total charge. Take advantage of your abilities in this area. Follow the suggestions given above, and take the time to go through this checklist before you consider yourself dressed to go.

CHECKLIST

1. Have I set my goals and objectives for the interview?
2. Do I know what type of image I want to project?
3. Do I know with whom I will be interviewing?
4. Have I chosen the appropriate clothing?
5. Am I wearing the best quality clothing I can afford?
6. Am I wearing clothing in which I am comfortable?
7. Am I clean and properly scented?
8. Is my make-up appropriate to my age, gender, and desired position?
9. Are my accessories of good quality and appropriate to the position?
10. Have I prepared my wardrobe and laid it out ready to go the night before the interview?

USING YOUR ADVANTAGES AND DISADVANTAGES

1. MATTERS CONSIDERED
2. LEGAL OR OTHER EFFECTS
3. UTILIZING OR CHANGING

With the variety of persons available for numerous positions within thousands of firms, each person is bound to have some characteristics that are advantageous or disadvantageous in a particular situation. While you may consider a particular aptitude or accomplishment or feature of yourself an advantage, the firm might view it negatively; on the other hand, something you have always secretly wanted to change about yourself may get you hired. The following materials will help you see what specific things might be viewed as advantages or disadvantages, and how to use them to their best effect.

Matters Considered

There are as many features or characteristics considered by employers as there are employers. However, there are several that are almost always a factor in whether or not a person is employed. Determine whether you have inherent advantages or disadvantages based on the following.

Your physical attributes. Physical attributes include your appearance (in many instances, not being stunningly attractive is more important than being stunningly attractive), your race, your gender, your age, and your handicaps. You should be aware that each of these factors is considered (at least subconsciously), so that you are able to maximize the positive impact.

Your background. Your background gives you advantages or disadvantages in such matters as religion, clubs and organizations you have joined, and schools you have attended. Knowing whether such matters are important to the firm to which you are applying will help you determine whether to emphasize or ignore a particular portion of your background.

Your matters of personal choice. A freedom of choice matter is one where you make the decision on your status. For example, employers might consider whether you are married or single, or whether you have children or not. They might consider your sexual preferences to be important. They might not legally be allowed to ask about such matters, but a skillful interviewer may easily get you talking until you let drop information you would rather not have said.

Legal or Other Effects

Now that you are aware of the considerations that might be advantages or disadvantages, think about the effects of those considerations. Consider the following.

Legal versus illegal discrimination. Some states still do not have laws prohibiting discrimination against homosexuals. Some states allow discrimination in certain positions due to gender. Be aware of whether or not you may be discriminated against due to your race, gender, age, sexual preferences, or other matters. When such discrimination is illegal, and you feel that you are being discriminated against solely on such a basis, you should attempt, if possible, to get proof of such discrimination during the interview for possible later legal action. Before you decide to pursue legal action, weigh the advantages and disadvantages carefully; job discrimination is often hard to prove.

The effect of making an honest statement regarding your advantages and disadvantages. You learned earlier in this book that doing homework on the background of the firm and those with whom you will be working is an excellent idea. Such homework allows you to determine whether you are likely to get the job because of a consideration (if you are all members of the same religion, for example) or unlikely to get such a position (the company has a tradition of not hiring those of your race or gender). Some attributes are obviously unable to be hidden (such as gender, age, or race), while others may be ignored or downplayed (such as religion, background, sexual preference).

Your willingness to change to make a disadvantage into an advantage. If you are able to change a characteristic, or if you are able to give the appearance of having changed, are you willing to do so? This question most frequently arises in connection with organizations or with families. You might be asked to join a particular organization with whose goals you disagree. You might be "expected" to work for a particular political party. Or you might be expected to live according to a particular moral code (for example, getting married rather than living together). Take the time to analyze how important the position is to you and how far you are willing to change to obtain it.

Utilizing or Changing

In the above passage, you were encouraged to think about changing yourself to turn a disadvantage into an advantage. This section discusses *not* changing yourself at all, but turning the disadvantage itself into an advantage. The following material will help you do so.

Show a governmental or legal advantage to your employment. If you take the time to do homework on affirmative action, you might find that companies are encouraged to hire minorities, or the handicapped. While the company is no doubt aware of this, your knowledge on the topic will impress the interviewer.

Show a need for a person with your characteristics. If you are of a different race or religion or have a different sexual preference than the majority of the people in the office, you could mention how you could gear your work towards those who are not represented or understood by the firm. Persons in positions dealing with the public have the leverage in this situation.

Don't worry whether an attribute or characteristic of yours is an advantage or a disadvantage; doing so is merely a waste of time. Rather, spend the time learning what might be positively or negatively viewed by the prospective employer, so that you are prepared to emphasize the advantages and make the best of the disadvantages. The following checklist will help.

CHECKLIST

1. How might my physical attributes help or hinder me?
2. How might my background affect my chances of employment?
3. Are my personal freedom of choice matters considered with my application?

4. Can I legally be discriminated against due to one of the above considerations?
5. Does the firm have a tradition of discrimination against those with my characteristics?
6. Can any attributes of mine be changed or be given the appearance of change?
7. Am I willing to change myself to eliminate a possible disadvantage?
8. Can I show a governmental or legal advantage to the firm that hires me?
9. Can I show a need for a person with my particular attributes?
10. Am I aware what characteristics of mine are obvious/able to be concealed?

During

YOU REALIZE HOW important an interview can be to your future success. You also realize that you probably will have only one chance to promote yourself, to convince the interviewer that you are the best person for the job. Therefore, the one thing you want to avoid is having to spend the day after the interview saying, "If only I had/ hadn't done that!"

During the interview, you are expected to be both the interviewee (the person being interviewed) and the interviewer (you want to find out what the company is offering you just as the company wants to find out what you are offering it). You may find that a great deal of conversation or activity is packed into a short meeting. This *during* section is written to help you understand and be prepared for many of the activities that may occur during the interview.

In this section, you will learn about the attitudes you should and should not display, and about the best way to use past employers. You will learn how to be prepared for discussions of money. You will be told about the common practice of being given an examination, and about touring the facilities. You will also learn how to extricate yourself from an interview gracefully when you decide that you don't want the job. In short, you will learn about many questions or situations you may encounter during an interview and how to handle them.

Not all the material in this section will be relevant to everybody. For example, in some interviews, no exams are given. If you are an attorney, it is highly unlikely that you will be asked to prove your legal knowledge. However, if you are a clerical worker, chances are you will be asked to take a skills test on the spot. Please read all the material. Even if you feel that one particular section is unlikely to apply to your individual situation, you will probably find some information there that will be useful to you.

During the interview, you will have much on your mind. Reading this material and accepting the relevant suggestions will help you be prepared and professional.

10 CRITICAL DO'S AND DON'TS OF INTERVIEWING

1. DON'T smoke or make a strong stand over the smoking/ non-smoking controversy. You are more likely to be hired if the interviewer feels that you will not create or contribute to problems between those who feel the office should exclude or isolate smokers and those who feel that smoking is the individual's right. Even if the interviewer is smoking, try to go without a cigarette for the duration of the conversation.

2. DON'T chew gum, candy, or breath mints. Having something in your mouth will make your words difficult to understand, and you will project a nonprofessional image. Get rid of anything you are chewing before you enter the reception area. Remember that the impression you make on people there counts too; make it a positive one.

3. DON'T fidget with your hair, jewelry, or clothing. Twirling your hair, smoothing your moustache, spinning a ring, or adjusting your tie will detract the interviewer's attention from what you are saying. You want to project the image of a relaxed, self-confident person.

4. DON'T take a drink ("for courage!") or a cold medicine containing an antihistamine just prior to going for the interview. The drink will show up on your breath and quite probably in your conversation and conduct. Antihistamines usually make a person drowsy; you want to be as sharp and alert as possible.

5. DON'T be late. Arriving even a few minutes late for a scheduled interview can leave a very negative impression, with both the interviewer and his or her secretary or receptionist. Being on time is both professional and courteous. Being punctual shows that you value the interviewer's time. On the other hand, don't make the interviewer feel guilty if he or she is late. Making the interviewer uncomfortable will not help your cause one bit.

6. DON'T swear, use slang, or attempt to impress the interviewer with esoteric jargon. Even if you are trying to be "just one of the guys," swearing will leave a negative impression. Swearing shows the interviewer that your vocabulary is so weak and your ideas so disorganized that you have to use curses to fill in the blanks. Using slang in an interview situation is undignified and is likely to be perceived as unprofessional. Using technical language with an interviewer (who often is not directly connected with the technical aspects of your job) rarely impresses the interviewer; instead you are likely to leave him or her with the impression that you were "showing off" or being pompous.

7. DON'T become overly familiar or gushing with the interviewer. While you want to establish a good rapport, you do not want to treat the interviewer as your long-lost friend. Be friendly but not unctuous. Most interviewers can readily spot insincere flattery.

8. DON'T constantly interrupt the interviewer; give him or her a chance to talk. While it's true that you will be expected to discuss yourself and your capabilities, and will have to answer questions, allow the interviewer to conduct the interview.

9. DON'T point out your weaknesses and faults unless directly asked. Never make excuses. Why call to the interviewer's attention a weakness that he or she might have missed? By stressing your weaknesses, you are sabotaging your own efforts. You might consider that you are being honest and above board; actually you are making the interviewer wonder why you bothered to come to the interview if you have so many faults.

10. DON'T evade questions or hedge your answers. While you do not want to volunteer too much negative information, you do want to answer questions directly and completely. Make certain that you understand what the interviewer wants to know, then supply that information

concisely but precisely. Don't try to second-guess the motive behind a question.

1. DO be prepared to answer a question on your smoking preferences. You quite likely will be asked whether you are a smoker or a non-smoker and how strongly you feel about working with others who do not share your preferences.

2. DO have fresh, clean breath. Chewing gum or a breath mint is not a bad idea, as long as you rid yourself of it before you enter the office. Check in a mirror to make absolutely certain that your teeth (or moustache) have no lingering bits of food or smudges of lipstick.

3. DO plan ahead on what to do with your hands. You might want to use them for gesturing (don't get carried away with wide sweeping gestures and knock the interviewer's papers right off his or her desk!) or you may want to keep them folded in your lap. If you know that you are the nervous type who usually fidgets constantly, carry a note pad or some other prop that you can hold inconspicuously.

4. DO be physically prepared for the interview. Eat a nutritious meal prior to the interview so that you will be physically alert. Get sufficient sleep the night before to allow you to look and feel your best. If the interview is going to be quite early in the morning, and you are not customarily an early riser, you may want to get up early the entire week before the interview, to get your body used to the change.

5. DO take the time prior to the interview to drive to the site, so that you know exactly how much time it will take you to arrive. Allow plenty of time for delays due to heavy traffic or adverse weather conditions. Make certain that you have allotted yourself sufficient time for preparation in the morning; even if you aren't late, having to rush to get ready will affect you negatively.

6. DO use words and terms with which you are familiar. Use your best grammar and diction. If you realize that you have poor speech patterns, do not try to excuse or explain them; simply do your best and be comfortable.

7. DO treat the interviewer with respect. You may be friendly and congenial without being insincere. You will be striking a balance between being hypocritically gushing and overly formal and pompous. Even if you feel that the interviewer has no idea what he or she is talking about, be polite. Never let your exasperation or irritation show.

8. DO listen carefully to what the interviewer has to say. Make certain that he or she has finished a sentence or a topic of discussion before you begin talking. Be careful not to spend so much time preparing what you are going to say in your own mind that you forget to listen to a new topic of conversation the interviewer has just introduced. Be especially careful not to answer rhetorical questions.

9. DO be prepared to explain or justify any weak areas. If you have left out periods of time on your resume, you are likely to be asked about your activities during those times. If you have switched jobs often, or have changed fields, be prepared with a rational, logical explanation of your actions.

10. DO be prepared to give specific answers to specific questions. From having read this book, you should be aware of the types of questions the interviewer is likely to ask you, so that you can prepare your answers ahead of time. Remember to bring any materials necessary with you. Be organized and have extra copies that the interviewer can keep.

THE PROPER ATTITUDE

1. SELLING YOURSELF
2. SELF-CONFIDENCE

3. PATIENCE
4. AMBITION

During the interview, you will undoubtedly be under some pressure. Although most interviewers are very good at putting applicants at their ease, many job seekers are uncomfortable and don't act naturally. Since the attitude you display is at least as important as the credentials you bring with you, take the time to go through the following materials.

Selling Yourself

The purpose of an interview is to allow you and the company to determine whether you wish to be associated with one another. Other sections of this book discuss your evaluation of the company's worth to you; this section stresses how you must "sell yourself" to the company.

Be aware of the qualifications necessary for the position. You must know what the firm is looking for before you can convince the interviewer that you are right for the job. Make certain that you have asked enough questions or done enough background research to know what specific education or experience is being sought in an employee.

Stress that you have the qualifications necessary for performing well in the position. There is no logic to knowing that you have the qualifications and not letting the interviewer share that knowledge. Take every opportunity to state *very specifically and in detail* that each requirement of the position meshes with one of your qualificaons. Take the time to give a detailed analysis, such as, "The position calls for a person with a knowledge of the computer language BASIC. Not only am I familiar with it, having programmed in it for several years, but I did my senior project in that language. I also taught BASIC programming when I was a graduate teaching assistant." In short, use the requirements as a checklist to go through with the interviewer.

Show the interviewer that you are unique and the best possible person for the position. Depending upon the job, there may be many persons who have the proper qualifications. Probably everyone who interviewed had at least the basic background and experience necessary. Therefore, you must make a special effort to convince the interviewer that you are unique and special. Emphasize some specific quality or bit of experience that makes you the best person for the job. Leave the interviewer with the idea that you meet and in some ways even *exceed* the requirements.

Self-Confidence

There is often a fine line between being self-confident and assured, and being aggressive and arrogant. Occasionally, applicants have the opposite problem: rather than being overly confident, they are insecure and come across as being timid. Try to strike a balance between the two.

Don't be too arrogant. You want to make certain that the interviewer is aware of your good qualities; you do not want to force him or her to acknowledge them verbally. Don't try so hard to impress the interviewer that you leave the impression you think you are smarter than he or she is. Also, be very certain not to contradict the interviewer.

Giving the interviewer your documentation (discussed earlier in this book) and answering his or her questions fully will allow him or her to understand how truly qualified you are. You do not want to keep on talking about your achievements and boasting of your abilities simply to get an acknowledgment from the interviewer. Normally, you will know when arrogance is alienating the interviewer; he or she will tend to withdraw or to change the subject.

Don't be overly critical. People don't like to hear their firm criticized. Most people follow the maxim that "I can complain about it, but no outsider should." Even if you have questions or criticisms that you must handle prior to accepting the position, make certain that you do so tactfully. Few people object to narrative questions spoken in a neutral tone, or to comments that are actually criticisms but are spoken rather diffidently or regretfully ("I really wish this otherwise excellent firm could offer a dental plan to its employees, don't you?").

No one wants to hear you criticize your past firms or employers either. When people hear you criticize others, they sometimes get the impression that you might as easily talk about them in the same manner. While you may feel very strongly about the "wrongs" you suffered, your complaints make a bad reflection on you. Try to keep a professional attitude when asked why you left your last position.

Don't talk too much. Often an applicant is nervous and just keeps chattering away. Practice answering the questions and letting the interviewer set the tone of the conversation. It is his or her job to elicit the necessary information in the alloted time; you do not want to talk so much that you make the appointment run long, or make it impossible for the interviewer to ask vital questions.

Don't be too aggressive. There is a difference between having a take-charge personality, and taking charge. You *do* want to seem confident and capable. You do *not* want to go into the interview and begin dictating what questions will and will not be asked. The interviewer has undoubtedly asked the same questions to many other applicants and has an interview format with which he or she is comfortable. Your changing that format could easily confuse or irritate the interviewer. Let him or her set the pace.

Be self-confident. The interviewer is accustomed to meeting nervous people. Do not worry if your hand shakes slightly, or if your voice quivers for the first few minutes of conversation. Interviewers are trained to ignore such matters. What the interviewer does not ignore is your self-assessment. If you project a confident manner, the interviewer will be more confident in your ability to perform well on the job. If you are diffident about your ability to do a job well, you will not get that job. This book has been written to enable you to be totally self-confident as you enter the interview, because you are prepared.

Patience

During the interview, you might be asked the same question over and over again. This might be an error on the part of the interviewer (who works with many people) or it might be a specific tactic testing your ability to work well in repetitive conditions.

Never lose your temper or be sharp with the interviewer. The interviewer is only doing his or her job. You must assume that he or she knows what is going on. Do not assume that you know better than the interviewer; remember that you are dependent at least partially on his or her goodwill. If you find that you are beginning to lose your temper, change the subject for a moment. Or take a short walk to the water cooler. Or cough and take some time to recover. Do anything to get away from your mounting irritation.

Many interviewers have the experience of dealing with the applicant who acts as if he is doing everyone a favor by being present. Even if you are totally convinced that the interviewer is doing a very poor job of questioning you, be respectful. Do not start sentences with such comments as, "As I just told you" or "As you can see on the documents I gave you." Fight the temptation to sigh or to exchange knowing glances with others who might be present. Never try to embarrass the interviewer in front of others.

On the other hand, there are times when you can be *too* patient. If you are applying for a position that requires special qualities, you may find that the interviewer intentionally baits you, goading you into losing your temper. If you take everything meekly and never assert yourself, you may not get the position. There are times when you must let the interviewer know that you are aware of his or her tactics and that it is time for you to take charge. Such "games-playing" is more likely to occur during role-playing interviews, when you are asked to pretend that you are the boss and the interviewer is the employee.

Ambition

The question of ambition is a very delicate one: you should show you are determined to improve yourself and the company, but not give the impression that you are out to take jobs away from others.

If you are going to be a salesperson, then by all means appear as ambitious as you are. Sales is a field calling for an aggressive, ambitious person. On the other hand, if you are going to be working as a clerk or a secretary or in another position where you will be less likely to receive a promotion, you may want to moderate your ambition. If the company is interviewing because all the other workers at a given position stayed for three months, then took what they'd learned and applied for a better position, it is probably wary of hiring one who might do the same thing. Even if that is your plan, try not to show your determination.

Your display of ambition should be realistic. If you are 21 years old, have no college degree and no experience, you may find that the interviewer finds your ambition rather difficult to accept. He or she might wonder why such an ambitious person has not bothered to finish school, or has not been able to get a job before. If you have no education, or few skills, and tell the interviewer that you want to be president of your own firm in three years, he or she might think that you are not able to assess a situation realistically. Although you know how hard you are willing to work, and how many fine qualities you have, the interviewer only sees the image you project. Tailor your ambitions and goals to impressive but realistic levels.

Attitude is partially a matter of your personality. If you are naturally a shy, retiring person, a little practice will not change you into a hearty and aggressive individual. However, you can take the time to consider certain facets of your attitude, and make certain that you are showing yourself to your best advantage. The following checklist will help.

CHECKLIST

1. Am I aware of the qualifications for the position, and am I stressing how I meet or exceed them?
2. Am I "selling myself" by emphasizing that I am unique and the best person for the job?
3. Am I too arrogant, alienating the interviewer by demanding acknowledgment of my abilities?
4. Am I too critical of this company or of my past firms?
5. Am I too prolix or aggressive, taking charge of the interview?
6. Am I not sufficiently confident?

7. Am I too short-tempered and sharp or too long-suffering?
8. Am I being too meek in a situation that calls for less patience and more action?
9. Does my job call for an ambitious person?
10. Are my ambitions realistic?

QUESTIONS YOU SHOULD EXPECT TO BE ASKED

Many interviewers have a stock of standard questions that they ask of virtually all job applicants. The well-prepared job seeker will have learned as many of those questions as possible and will have taken the time to think out the answers prior to going in for the interview.

While there are hundreds of questions, some casual, some probing and specific, that you could be asked in the course of an interview, there are thirteen basic questions that seem to be asked of everyone applying for any type of job. Take the time to read over the following questions and suggested answers. Note that the answers here are general; you should take the time to be specific and think about *your* answers, based on *your* goals and those of the firm.

1. Why do you want to work for this specific firm? Homework is invaluable to you for answering this question. By the time you get to the interview, you will have found out specifics that you can state to the interviewer, such as the fact that the company is noted for its state-of-the-art laboratory equipment, or for its close work with advanced government projects. You will be able to tell the interviewer that you are impressed with the low turnover rate, indicating employee satisfaction. You will be able to state that you respect the caliber of the staff with which you will be working, or that you like the goals and ambitions of the company. Be absolutely certain that you have spent enough time thinking about your answer to this question to be able to give SPECIFICS as to why this particular firm, over all the others in the field (and most probably there will not be that much difference between firms, realistically speaking; you will have to find one or two particular points to emphasize) was your first choice.

2. *Where do you want to be professionally in 1 year? 5 years? 10 years? 20 years?* This is a favorite question of all interviewers. Your answer to such a question tells much about you. The interviewer will be able to tell how ambitious you are, how determined and motivated you are. Again, use your homework to help you answer the question. Research the firm to determine what its short- and long-range goals are. If you note that it seems to be moving into high technology, state that you hope to obtain a degree in a high-tech field and work with sophisticated equipment. If the firm appears to be diversifying, state that you want to learn about several fields so that you can manage or work with persons in various areas. Be realistic when you answer this question. You do not want to tell the interviewer that in one year you want to have your Ph.D. and be managing your own division if that is an unrealistic goal. Take the time to think about your personal goals in relation to the firm's goals, and mesh the two to your advantage. An interviewer is likely to be inclined towards hiring a person whose goals fit those of the firm.

3. *What are your qualifications for this job? What makes you the best person for the job?* This question allows you to flood the interviewer with your skills and education and impress him or her with your capabilities. This is no time to be modest. You should of course have prepared any documentation (such as your resume, letters of recommendation, or merit reviews) to give to the interviewer to support your claims. However, this question calls for specifics. You want to think about what the job needs, then mention to the interviewer how your skills in those areas perfectly fill the needs. If the job involves dealing with the public, stress any experiences you have had working with people in a courteous and professional manner. If the job requires meeting deadlines, tell how you often worked evenings and weekends at school or in another job to make certain that the work was done on time. You must give specifics of why you, rather than another person with your same degrees, background, and work

experience, should be hired. Often such specifics include extracurricular activities, volunteer work, or just personal attributes. Again, know what the job calls for, then take the time to prepare an argument showing how you have those qualifications. You may also want to stress that you should be hired because you sincerely are excited about working for *this* company, and would be both loyal and enthusiastic.

4. What are your personal strengths? This question calls for much the same information as the previous one; however, the information should be presented in a totally different way. In the question regarding why you should be hired, you were to give specifics linking you with the position. In this question, you can be more general and show your overall sterling qualities, such as honesty, integrity, determination/motivation, capacity for hard work, etc. Take the time to think about four or five of your best qualities. You do not want to give the interviewer a long list of every good quality that every person aspires to. You want to emphasize those traits that are your *own* strongest points, especially those that you think the firm is seeking in a candidate for the job.

5. What are your personal weaknesses? This question should be approached with great care. You must walk a fine line between criticizing yourself in a constructive manner and telling the interviewer all your faults and foibles. Choose two points that you feel could use work and plan a short discussion of each. For example, you might state that you tend to be impatient. Note that this "weakness" actually could be construed as a strength. You allow the interviewer to infer that you are accustomed to working quickly and efficiently, so that you are impatient with yourself and others when a project is not done on time. You are actually turning a weakness into a strength. Another example of a point to discuss is perfectionism; state that you tend to be overly critical, a perfectionist. Again, such a fault could be a strength in a position that calls for specific tolerances and much detail work. Take the time to think about faults or weaknesses that the company could "help" you change into strong selling points.

6. Do you consider yourself a leader or a follower? The interviewer is really trying to determine your self-image. Of course he expects that you will be attempting to tell him what he wants to hear. If you are interviewing for a position as a manager, he knows that you will state that you view yourself as a leader. Your answer must be made memorable and distinct from those of all the other applicants by giving specifics. Tell exactly what experiences you have had in the past as a leader that have contributed to your self-concept. Discuss those personality traits you have that exhibit leadership potential.

7. What do you expect to get from the firm? Do not give the same answer to this question as you did to the "What are your goals in 1–5–10–20 years?" question. The interviewer here wants to know whether your expectations are realistic, whether you know what you want and demand from a company. Choose three to five benefits that you hope to obtain. For example, you might state that you are looking for an intellectual challenge or that you want to enhance your expertise or leadership abilities. Another example is that you want to be able to obtain on-the-job training on specific machinery or in certain fields or concepts. Whatever answer you choose, make certain that it is something that shows the interviewer that you know what you want for your professional future and have selected this company to help you obtain your goals.

8. Would you be willing to relocate or to change your job description in the future? This question is actually asking how flexible you are. If you have no objection to relocating, say so. If you are vehemently opposed to relocating, you personally will have to make the decision on whether or not to state that you have no objections. Certainly, you will probably increase your chances of being hired if the company thinks that you would relocate; however, if you are hired with that understanding and then refuse to relocate later, you could find yourself both out of a job and the recipient of much ill-feeling. If you do not want to relocate, you might want to tell the interviewer that you are willing to consider the question should it arise and should the opportunity offered by relocation be sufficient to merit the upheaval.

Such an answer has not closed the door on the discussion, but has not obligated you either.

When you are asked whether you would be willing to change your job description, the interviewer again is testing how flexible you can be. If the company is expanding or diversifying, it is probably looking for persons who will change with it. You have little to lose by stating that you would be willing to change your job description or duties; often such changes are for the better as you get increased and varied knowledge and experience.

9. *What would make you unhappy on the job?* This question does not call for your telling the interviewer all your pet peeves and irritations. He does not want to know that muzak drives you crazy or that you refuse to sit in the same room with someone who talks to himself. Take this opportunity to tell the interviewer any specific areas that you have had problems with in the past. For example, you might state that you would be unhappy on a job that required you to punch a time clock, and work exact hours. (Of course, you would *never* make a statement like this unless you had previously determined that this job did *not* require that you work specific hours. *Never* trap yourself by stating that you would be made unhappy by a situation that cannot be rectified.) Perhaps you prefer a less structured environment that lets you work when you want, as long as the work is done. You might state that you would be unhappy if you were not given sufficient autonomy and decision-making responsibility (note again how this could be stretched to mean that you are ambitious and an asset to the company, as you can work well on your own). Think about major, professional irritations (as opposed to personal, minor ones) and have a reasoned analysis prepared on why such matters would make you unhappy, and how you would rectify the situation. By all means never state that something that is unchangeable ("I don't like to work in an air-conditioned building") would make you unhappy. Always be prepared to give at least tentative solutions to any problems.

10. *What will you do if you are not offered this position?* This has been a popular question recently. Your answer should show that you

would try to increase your experience or further your education else-where, then apply again. You might state that you would continue your education, taking specific classes that would help you with the job in the future. You might state that you would accept a job with another firm to gain more experience in the field. Whatever you choose for an answer, make it very clear that this position is your first choice and that you will do everything possible to ensure receiving it.

11. Why did you leave your last job/why do you want to leave your current job? Do not use this question as an invitation to tell the interviewer all your troubles. As discussed previously, complaining reflects more poorly on you than on anyone else. Prepare specific, well-reasoned, logical answers. You might state that you changed industries, moved to another state or locale where the first business couldn't offer you work, or decided to look for a position where you could utilize your skills more fully. When answering this question, be certain to make yourself appear to be a person who always moves up in the job market, not one who simply moves laterally.

12. What were your major accomplishments/disappointments on your last job? You will have with you any documentation telling of specific accomplishments of which you are proud; when this question is asked, produce it for the interviewer to read. If you do not have any doc-umentation, have an answer prepared that states three or four basic accomplishments that show your best qualities. You could state that you are proud of having finished an important project on time and under budget. You might state that you were pleased to win the efficiency award or boast the highest sales record. Another answer may be that the department you managed had the lowest employee turnover rate in the company. Be specific in those accomplishments you mention.

Discussing disappointments can be difficult. You do not want to whine or complain and make it seem as if all your disappointments were caused by others; on the other hand, you do not want to tell stories that make you look inefficient. State that you were disap-pointed that you were unable to expand your department due to budget cuts, or that you had wanted to be able to give merit raises to those you felt were deserving. You may state that you felt you could have done an improved job on a specific project given more time or equipment. Again, make your answer to this question show that you were disappointed in yourself only because you so desperately wanted to do well for the firm.

13. *What were your specific duties in your last job?* This is the simplest question. You probably had a job description that you can simply use to give an answer. If no such description existed, take a two-step approach to your answer. First, give those overall duties and responsibilities that you were given on a long-term basis (such as finishing a specific project). Second, give an example of your day-to-day duties, such as monitoring the work of others, keeping payroll records, marking inventory.

If you can predict the questions that you will be asked, and take the time to create logical, professional, well-reasoned answers to those questions, your preparation will show. You personally will feel more relaxed and less helpless. The interviewer will be left with the impression of a person who knows his or her goals and aspirations, understands his or her strengths and weaknesses, and in general is knowledgeable and thoughtful. The following checklist should be consulted to help you prepare your answers.

CHECKLIST

1. Why am I interested in working for this particular firm?
2. What are my professional goals for the next 1/5/10/20 years?
3. What is unique or special about me that places me above all the other applicants for this position?
4. What are my personal strengths that would best benefit the firm?
5. What are my personal weaknesses that could be construed as more helpful than harmful?
6. Am I a leader or a follower and what has made me so?

7. What do I expect to get from this firm?
8. Am I willing to relocate or to change my position in the future?
9. What would make me unhappy at work?
10. What are my future plans if I am not offered a position with this firm?
11. Why did I leave my last job/why am I anticipating leaving my current job?
12. What were my major accomplishments/disappointments on my last job?
13. What were my specific duties in my last job?

QUESTIONS YOU SHOULD ASK DURING THE INITIAL INTERVIEW

You may have many questions that you want to ask of the interviewer. In order to make a good impression, during the initial interview you should ask only those questions that emphasize your desire to work for the company. In other words, ask only what you can do for your company, not what your company can do for you. In a later section of this book, you will be given suggestions on questions to ask *after* you have been offered the job. Those questions will cover topics more personal to you.

During the interview, you should have a list of questions ready to be asked. If you intend simply to ask questions as you think of them, or as the interview gets to the right topic, you may find yourself leaving without the information you wanted. Having no questions at all may give the interviewer the impression that you aren't really interested in the job, and asking too many or the wrong kinds of questions may make you sound like a prosecuting attorney. The following materials will help you determine the kinds of questions to ask.

1. What is my job title and description? Find out exactly (if possible) what your title will be and what duties it entails. In most firms, written job descriptions are available that will help you find out what you are responsible for accomplishing.

2. What qualifications is the firm looking for in the employee? This question should allow you to learn exactly what degrees, classes, or general education is mandatory and which is suggested or desired for the person who will be holding this position. You should also learn what experience is necessary: must you have knowledge of particular machinery or equipment, familiarity with specific languages, procedures, concepts? Try to learn as much as possible about the "ideal" employee that the company has in mind.

3. What specific responsibilities and duties does the position entail? This is one of the most critical questions you can ask. Before you know whether you will accept the position or not, you must be aware of what you will be required to do, both on a daily and a long-term basis. Ask sufficiently detailed and pointed questions to ensure that you know *exactly* what your responsibilities are, from report generating, to hiring and firing, to meeting with clients. While most firms provide something called a "job description," such a description may be a short (one or two sentence) overview of the position (e.g., "selling and reordering inventory"). You must obtain more specific information. Note that the more information you receive, the more you will learn about what the firm is really looking for. You may be able to see that one attribute or experience of yours that you felt was irrelevant is in fact important and a good selling point.

4. What are the possibilities for a promotion? Do not think that you will seem overly ambitious if you ask about a promotion before you have even gotten the job. Especially if you are applying for an entry-level position, you should give the impression of one who wants to improve and move up within the organization. Ask what types of moves are possible and how long it usually takes to receive a promotion.

You should realize that an initial interview is primarily for the company's benefit; the interviewer's responsibility is to determine whether you are qualified for the position. *After* you have been offered the job, the second interview—if there is one—is primarily for your benefit. It is during that second interview that you may want to ask the many questions that are important to your personal interests. (Those questions may be found in a later section of this book.)

Before you go to the initial interview, have your questions prepared. Review the following checklist for help.

CHECKLIST

1. What is my exact job title and description?
2. What qualifications is the firm looking for in the employee?
3. What are the exact, specific duties inherent in the position?
4. What are the possibilities for a promotion?

USING PAST EMPLOYERS

1. LETTERS OF REFERENCE
2. PERMISSION TO CONTACT (PRO/CON)
3. NEGATIVE FEELINGS
4. OMISSIONS
5. NUMEROUS POSITIONS OF SHORT DURATION

During the interview, the subject of your past employment is almost certain to arise. You will have to decide before going into the interview how you will handle that subject. The following material will introduce you to the concepts you will want to consider regarding your past employers.

Letters of Reference

Most prospective employers do not ask for letters of reference; such letters are generally used only in academic situations (such as when you are trying to get into a special school or program). However, occasionally either you or the prospective employer will want to use such letters. In those instances, consider the following guidelines.

Make certain that the letters you are supplying are relevant. You do not want to produce letters telling what a wonderful nurse you were when you are now applying for a position as a plumber. A letter of reference should discuss those qualities you showed on your last job that you feel your new employer is seeking. If the letter discusses general concepts, such as professionalism, punctuality, and enthusiasm for the job, bring it with you. Those qualities are important in any position. However, if the letter merely tells what a wonderful scrub nurse you were with all your technical information, it is not relevant and should not be produced.

Make certain that the letters you are supplying are impressive. If you are going to spend the interviewer's time on a letter, make absolutely certain that it is sufficiently impressive to remain in his mind. A letter from your co-workers or from someone other than the top person is not very impressive. Try to obtain a letter from the president of the firm, or from the highest ranking officer you can find, written on official letterhead stationery.

Bring only letters that are legitimate. Some people write their own letters. They assume that no one will be the wiser. They "borrow" a few sheets of letterhead stationery and type up what they want said. But be warned: many industries are small, self-contained worlds, with someone always knowing the very person with whom you are concerned. It is rarely worth the risk to your reputation to write your own letter. Of course, if the person whom you ask for a reference agrees that you should write the letter and simply have him or her acknowledge it, that is a different matter. Often, persons who are asked to write many reference letters try to save time by doing just that.

Permission to Contact (Pro/Con)

In the vast majority of cases, there is no contact between past and prospective employers. However, during the interview you might be asked to sign a release form, allowing the firm to contact your past employers to verify information you have stated. Be prepared to decide whether to allow such contact.

Consider the possibility that refusing to allow contact will jeopardize your chances of employment. If you do not sign the release, the company may not (legally) contact your former employer and your former employer may not (legally) release information on you. Some companies simply refuse to process an application that does not have this accompanying release. If you are very concerned that contacting your past employer will produce a negative result, or if you refuse to sign the release as a matter of principle, discuss the effect of such a refusal with the interviewer. Be prepared to accept the consequences by understanding them fully.

If your application form told nothing but the unembellished truth, and if your past employers are likely to retain fond memories of your work, by all means sign the release. In most instances, the contact between the two firms is limited to a short telephone call or letter asking for a verification of employment dates, salary, and reason for leaving.

On the other hand, if you decided to "emphasize" your past salary a little, or exaggerated the importance of your former position, you might consider refusing to sign the release. It is usually better to refuse to sign the release than to take a chance that you will be found to have lied or exaggerated.

Negative Feelings

If you and your former employer parted with a good deal of rancor, you will have a difficult situation to handle during future interviews. You will have to decide how to discuss your past employment without leaving an impression of yourself as a troublemaker or a complainer.

Determine whether there was a logical cause for the ill will. If you left your last position because you were promised a raise that was never awarded, you have a valid reason for the departure and should bring it up during the interview. Even if you left after shouting and screaming at the boss, the accountants, and your secretary, you will have an excuse (or at least a rationalization) of such behavior that most people will recognize. There is no need to discuss your anger; simply mention that the ill will occurred when a promise to you was not fulfilled.

Avoid overemphasizing the negativity. No one wants to hire a person who speaks ill of his or her past employers. If you tell a total stranger of all your problems and negative feelings towards your last firm, the interviewer knows that you may do the same about any firm. If you are forced to discuss the ill will that occurred on your past job (for example, you might think it wise to mention it if you know this firm will have to contact your past firm for references), mention it briefly, giving logical reasons for it, and then move on to another topic. Do not waste the interviewer's time with discussions of personality clashes and with trying to justify your behavior.

Omissions

There may be times when you will want to omit a previous job from your resume entirely. Or there may have been times when you were not working, so that your resume shows a gap in your work history.

Determine whether you will gain from not listing certain positions. If you worked twenty years as a pilot, were laid off and worked as a teacher for six months, then were hired again as a pilot, you probably do not need to mention your teaching experience. If you took several years out of your career to pursue a different occupation, you should mention it, but briefly. The main reason not to mention a position is that it shows that you were demoted, or were in some way working at a position that would reflect negatively on your integrity, abilities, or professionalism. However, make certain that if you do not list such positions, you have decided how to answer any questions about the gap in your employment.

Consider what statement you will make regarding the length of time between jobs. You might have taken a few years off to be with your family, to begin a business of your own, to return to school, to recover from an illness, or simply to relax. In such an instance, you will not have a position to list on your resume, leaving a gap of a year or more. If the interviewer asks you what you were doing during such a time, make sure that you have considered your answer carefully. You may want to tell the truth, wholly and without exaggeration—or you may want to rewrite a few facts to make them look more professional. No one is suggesting that you lie on your resume, but you may want to list your unemployed time as a period when you were "self-employed." Often, a good listing is that you were a consultant or a free-lance worker.

Numerous Positions of Short Duration

If you have gone from one job to another and have not held any one position for a length of time, you may find that such "job shopping" works against you. The following considerations should help you prepare for any questions or negative feelings that such a record creates.

Is job switching common or uncommon in this industry? In some fields, it is the rule rather than the exception to go from job to job. If you are in construction you probably work less than a year on any one project. Some people are fortunate enough to be in fields where the worker is more in demand than the job. People working with computers often switch jobs yearly, moving to better positions with more responsibility and higher salaries. If you are in such a field, you need not worry about the impression your numerous jobs will make on the interviewer; he or she will understand.

If you are in a field where job switching is not common and is frowned upon, you should determine your explanation of why you have so frequently switched. Do not fall into the trap of blaming others and whining and rationalizing; try to give legitimate reasons for all of your transfers. You can always discuss such factors as location (a desire to move to a new city, or even to a new part of the city), family pressures (an additional child, making it necessary to look for a higher-paying job), or job motivation (you wanted to gain the knowledge and experience offered by the new job).

Determine whether you should *not* include some jobs on your resume. As mentioned before, there might be a time when you feel that it would be to your advantage not to include certain positions on your resume. As a rule, any job you have worked at for less than six months may be deleted. Of course, if the nature of the job were such that it necessarily lasted less than six months (you were hired to create a specific plan or project) you should include it. Do not be afraid to list all of your positions, emphasizing that the variety of work has left you with an abundance of different experiences. Turn a possible defect into a virtue by stressing how flexible you are.

Before you go into the interview, decide how you will handle any questions that arise regarding your past employment or your former employers. Decide whether you want your employer contacted or not, whether you will produce letters of reference, how you will handle short-term positions. In the matter of former employment, as in most other matters during an interview, being prepared for all possibilities will help you be in control, self-assured, and professional. The following checklist will help you prepare.

CHECKLIST

1. Do I have letters of reference that are relevant to the new position?
2. Do I have letters of reference that are both legitimate and impressive?
3. What will be the effect of my refusing to allow the new firm to contact my past employers?
4. Should I allow the new firm to contact my past employers?
5. Were there logical or rational causes for any ill will between myself and my former employer?
6. Am I overemphasizing the negativity of my past employers?
7. Should I leave certain past jobs off my resume?
8. How will I explain the time intervals between jobs?
9. Is my new position in an industry where job switching is common and accepted?
10. How will I justify my numerous job changes?

TAKING AN EXAMINATION

> 1. PREPARATION
> 2. REFUSING TO PARTICIPATE
> 3. ANALYSIS OF THE RESULTS

Depending on the type of job you are applying for, you may be required to take some sort of an examination as a part of the interview. The exam may be substantive, testing that you are capable of doing the work. For example, if you are applying for a position as a typist, it is common to have you do a timed typing test. If you are applying for a position as a chemist, you may have to take a short multiple-choice exam testing your knowledge of chemistry. Or the exam may also be an aptitude examination. You may have to take an exam that simply asks you which of the following activities you would prefer to do on a weekend, requiring you to choose from among several alternatives. Such exams are used for personality profiles and possible job reassignments.

Finally, you may be asked to take a lie detector (polygraph) examination. If you are applying for a position as a security guard, or as a worker in a defense firm, you probably will be asked to take such an exam. It consists only of your being attached to a machine called a polygraph and being asked questions. Your reactions to the questions are charted by the polygraph; such reactions are then read by a trained operator to determine the truthfulness of your answers. A review of the following materials will help you be prepared for any of the above types of examinations.

Preparation

If you know that you will be asked to participate in an examination, or if you suspect that you will be, you should be prepared. If possible, try to speak with others in the firm to ask them what the exam covers. Occasionally, the interviewer will be willing to mail you a brochure on the exam before the interview takes place.

If the exam is a skills test, such as a timed typing sample, you can practice at home. Do so under actual test circumstances; that is, pretend that you are taking the exam under the eye of the interviewer. Do not stop to get a cup of coffee, or stop and start again. If the exam is a competency test, requiring you to answer questions testing your knowledge of certain subjects, take a few hours to review the basics of those subjects. You probably have some study guides or textbooks left from your courses; if not, the library will have materials you can use. Have a relative or friend ask you questions until you are confident and knowledgeable.

Refusing to Participate

You may decide that you want the job, but you do not think you should have to take an examination to prove yourself. This situation often occurs when persons are asked to submit to a polygraph test; also, some persons who are experienced in a given field feel that they are being insulted by being asked to take a simple skills test. Before telling the interviewer that you refuse to take the exam, clear yourself on the following points.

Know why you are refusing. Are you refusing because you are afraid you will not pass the exam? Are you refusing because you feel the exam is an insult to you? Are you refusing on general principles? Before you decide to refuse, make certain that you have analyzed your reasons for the refusal and that they are logical.

Explain to the interviewer why you are refusing. A brusque refusal will leave a very negative impression on the interviewer. If you know why you will not take the exam, tell the interviewer. Explain your reasons logically and coherently, but do not be defensive and hostile. The interviewer probably has had many people refuse to take the exam; you are not the first. He or she will respect you for telling your reasons; however, do not say anything negative such as, "I don't think I could pass without studying more" or "I didn't realize that you wanted me to take a test!" Such a comment makes you look unprepared and incompetent.

Be prepared to offer an alternative or accept the effects of your refusal. If you are rejecting the exam because the timing is wrong, you might be able to ask for a delay, and take the exam later. If you are certain that you never will take the exam, be prepared to be rejected in favor of another equally well-qualified applicant who did take the exam. While there are some questions over the legality of refusing a position to a person *only* because he or she refused to take an examination (especially in the case of a lie-detector exam), generally an applicant will not win such a case. Remember that you are right to stand up for your principles, but that the company is looking out for its best interests as well.

Analysis of the Results

You probably will be told right on the spot how you did on the exam (unless the exam was a lengthy one, or an essay that must be graded carefully). You must be prepared to deal with both a positive and a negative result.

If you didn't pass the exam, the interviewer might be willing to let you repeat the exam at a later date, especially if it were obvious that you were unprepared. Before you agree to do so, be certain that you will study for it and could pass it on the second try. Otherwise you are wasting your time and that of the interviewer.

But suppose that you passed the exam, but just barely. While you might have many reasons for such a poor performance, fight the temptation to rationalize and make excuses to the interviewer. Accept your score, determine whether you want to take the exam again in an attempt to improve it, and do not try to justify yourself with excuses.

If you did extremely well, you want to maximize the effects of the exam. You will want to call the results to the attention of your prospective superiors. Try to get the test results in writing. If you are not hired for the job, you will have a written record of your score, should you later decide to contest your rejection. You might also use that score when applying to another firm.

While not all firms require that workers take exams during an interview, enough companies do to make it worth your while to be aware of the possibility. Before you go to the interview, go over the following checklist to help you be prepared.

CHECKLIST

1. Can I find out what style of test will be given?
2. Can I find out what material will be tested?
3. Can I study or practice for the test?
4. Do I know why I am refusing to take the exam?
5. Have I explained coherently to the interviewer my reasons for refusing to take the exam?
6. Can I offer an alternative to my taking the exam?
7. Am I prepared to accept the effects of my refusing to take the exam?
8. Could I repeat the exam if I didn't pass it or if I did poorly on it?
9. How can I use an excellent score to help me obtain the position?
10. How can I use an excellent score to my advantage in the future, with other firms?

OBSERVING THE FACILITIES

You should be observant of all that is around you as you go to and from the interview. While in most instances you will not be given a full-scale tour of the plant or the office site on your first interview, you probably will have the opportunity to walk through a part of the facilities on your way to the interviewer's office. Take the time and effort to gain as much knowledge of the physical plant and to get a feeling of the overall attitude of the employees as possible in that short time. There are specific considerations of which you should be aware.

Note the overall cleanliness and neatness of the facility. How well-kempt the premises are says much about the pride that the firm has in itself and in its image. If you can see at a glance that the grounds are beautifully landscaped and the buildings are sparkling clean, you know that the company pays attention to detail and that you may enjoy working in such an attractive setting.

Try to notice the security arrangements. If you notice that there is not good lighting in the parking lot, or that the parking lot is not easily visible from the main building, you may assume that there could be security problems with vandalism or theft or even assault on employees as they go to and from their cars.

Look for the general level of sophistication of the facilities and office equipment. If you notice that the receptionist is typing on a manual typewriter and that the Xerox machine appears to be ten years old, you have an indication that this firm does not spend a great deal of money on state-of-the-art equipment. If you intend to work at a position where the equipment is critical to your job performance, you may want to get assurances that the materials and equipment you need will be supplied.

You should, even in a very brief time, be able to get a general feeling of the comfort of the site. While all facilities seem to have occasional problems with the air conditioning and heating, you should see whether the office temperature is generally comfortable. Also, have items been provided for the comfort of the employees? Little things such as comfortable chairs and good lighting will probably affect you greatly on a day-to-day basis.

Finally and most importantly, try to gauge the overall employee attitude and morale. By observing the demeanor of the workers, from the first person who greets you to those by whom you pass on your way to meet with the interviewer, you can determine how happy and content the workers are. Of course, it is normal for workers to complain about a job, but if there is a feeling of camaraderie in the complaints at the water cooler, you may assume that the atmosphere is generally friendly.

In brief, make the most of any opportunity for observation that you may have. Remember that observing the site and facilities can give you an overall feeling for the type of firm for which you will be working. Getting an impression and acting on it now may save you unhappiness later.

WHEN YOU DON'T WANT THE JOB

     1. DETERMINING WHY
     2. ASKING FOR A VARIATION
     3. DELAY
     4. FOLLOW-UP LETTERS

During an interview, there may come a point when you realize that this position, no matter how much you thought you wanted it originally and no matter how hard you struggled to get the interview, is not for you. When you come to this conclusion, you must find a graceful way to acquaint the interviewer with your decision.

Determining Why

You must determine why you don't want the job. Since you have gone to a great deal of trouble to get and go through the interview, and since the company has taken the time and effort to interview you, you owe it to yourself and the firm to make certain that your decision is reasonable. Consider which of the following is your reason for rejecting the job.

You don't like the interviewer's personality. You may not like the interviewer. He or she may strike you as overly aggressive, or as incompetent and feeble. However, remember that you may not be working with or for the interviewer. Chances are, once you begin work, you will never see or hear from that person again. In a case like this, do not let a personality clash with the interviewer color your decision on whether to accept the job. But if you *will* be working for the interviewer and don't like him or her, it may save you a lot of pain later if you trust your instincts.

You are uncomfortable with yourself today. Everyone has an "off" day. Perhaps you are uncomfortable due to an illness, or a lack of sleep, or just sheer nervousness. Being irritable and uncomfortable during an interview is not sufficient reason to reject a position. Try to find the causes of your discomfort; if they are not job-related, try to reconsider your decision to reject the position.

You don't like the duties and responsibilities. This is probably the best reason to reject a job. If you have a true understanding of the duties and responsibilities inherent in the job, and you know what will be expected of you, and if you don't believe you are able to fulfill those expectations or simply don't want to fulfill them, then you would be doing the right thing by refusing the job.

Your "instincts" tell you to. Instincts or intuition may be based on many factors, some rational, some not. Sometimes what you call your "intuition" is really an excellent analysis, done in a split second, of the surroundings and the people. When you are tempted to reject a job due to a "gut reaction," take the time to analyze the validity of those factors that created such a reaction.

Asking for a Variation

Occasionally, you might be tempted to reject the job for one reason or another, but feel that a slight variation in the terms (e.g., in the salary or in your job description) would convince you to accept the position.

Before asking for a variation, make certain that your requests are reasonable. If you make a request that is totally unreasonable and that the interviewer absolutely cannot fulfill or accede to, he or she will know that you do not want the job but simply do not have the courage to say so. Then you are in effect insulting the intelligence of the interviewer and wasting his or her time. Make certain that your requests are logical and possible to fulfill.

Be sure that you will be willing to accept the job if your requests are granted. If you make a request, the interviewer will probably have to do some work to get it granted. If it is granted and you then reject the job anyway, you have wasted everyone's time and probably made the interviewer look foolish. Be certain that you are willing to consider accepting the position should the new conditions please you.

Make your requests specific and understandable. Communication is the key. If you do not tell the interviewer exactly what you want changed, he or she cannot be expected to read your mind. Make your requests specific, giving exact amounts when necessary (as with salaries or bonuses). Do not waste the interviewer's time by making vague requests that cannot be understood sufficiently to be granted.

Delay

You have decided that you want to delay your decision on whether to accept the job. How do you state this to the interviewer without actually rejecting the job for good? You may want to find a way to wait until you have decided to accept or reject another position for which you have interviewed.

If you want to delay your decision, consider whether you are being fair to the interviewer and the other applicants. Remember that while you are delaying, no one else is being offered the position. No one else is working at that position, which results in a hardship on the firm itself and perhaps on the current employees who are working two jobs rather than one. If you ask for time to consider the offer, make certain that you are doing so out of a sincere desire to think about the offer, not because you do not have the courage to tell the interviewer "no."

Tell the interviewer exactly how long you want to consider the offer. Be specific. Then say exactly why you want or need that much time. The interviewer will be more likely to grant you the delay if he or she can explain to the boss why such a delay was given. Be certain also to recognize that granting you a delay is a favor; *ask* for a delay rather than demand one.

Follow-up Letters

When you have absolutely decided to reject the job, you want to write a letter stating exactly why you are declining the position and thanking everyone concerned. There is a sample rejection letter in the appendix of this book. Following are some guidelines for such a letter.

Clearly state your reasons for declining the position. Do not write a vague, general letter stating that you do not want the job. Be certain to tell exactly why you do not want the position. If you simply don't like the position, give at least one specific reason; you might say that you don't want to travel so far to work every day, or that you want a company with a dental plan.

Be courteous throughout. You never know when the interviewer from this company might show up as the head of personnel at another company with which you interview. Always be certain to thank the interviewer for his or her time and effort. You want to leave an impression of yourself as a responsible, polite, professional person.

Try to make sure the door is left open for you for future possibilities. In many industries, persons shift jobs frequently. This is especially true in the "workers' market" industries such as computers and engineering. You want your letter to express your disappointment that you cannot accept the job *at this time*. Such a letter leaves open the possibility that you will be available in the future.

If you receive offers from more than one firm, you must decline some. Doing so with style requires that you have thought the matter out beforehand. Take the time to consider your decision carefully and frame your rejection professionally. Follow the suggestions outlined above, and go through the checklist that follows.

CHECKLIST

    1. Do I know why I want to reject the job?
    2. Is my reason for rejecting the job rational?
    3. Could any factors make me willing to accept the job?
    4. Am I willing to accept the job if a variation is granted?
    5. Are my requests for variations reasonable and specific?

6. Do I need a delay to determine my decision?
7. Have I explained my specific reasons for asking for a delay?
8. Have I written a courteous follow-up letter?
9. Has the letter given my specific reasons for rejecting the position?
10. Have I left open the possibility of future employment?

SALARY

1. SALARY HISTORY
2. MARKET WORTH
3. SALARY AMOUNT
4. BROACHING THE TOPIC

Salary is of primary importance to many people. Others weigh the importance of salary with a number of other factors such as benefits, experience to be gained, prestige, and potential for future growth. Whatever your goals regarding salary and benefits, you should have them clear in your mind before the interview. The following material will help you plan your research before the interview and the questions you want to ask during the interview. There are, however, several financial considerations that are important to discuss but which should not be raised at the initial interview. Such subjects should be considered after you have been offered the job but before you accept it. A full discussion of those topics is given in a later section.

Salary History

Unless you received an inordinately high salary at your previous position, you probably do not have a salary figure listed on your resume. Occasionally, you will have an application form that asks for "salary outline or guidelines." This means that the firm wants to know how little you will accept. The wise applicant merely fills in the standard sentence: "Salary to be negotiated." Listing a minimum salary could backfire, as one that is too low would make the company lose respect for you, while one that is too high may not get you an interview.

If your past salaries have been comparable to what you are asking for now, by all means discuss them. If you are asking for a salary that is much higher than you have had in the past, do not give your previous salaries.

Job applicants are often tempted to "inflate" their past salaries, telling the interviewer that they had earned more in the past than they actually did. Ethical considerations apart (you are the only one who can determine how strongly you feel about the lies you will tell), you must think of whether you will be found out in a lie (or exaggeration). Since many industries are small, with much socializing or doing business with other firms, chances are you could be discussed and your untruth discovered. Even if such is not the case, you may find that your conscience bothers you and that you are constantly in fear of being found out. Think carefully before deciding to exaggerate a salary.

Often you will be given a release form to sign that allows an interviewer to contact the accounting branch of your last business to find out your salary. If you don't want it known, do not sign such a release. You may gracefully decline to sign; there is no need to be belligerent or defensive.

Market Worth

You should have done enough research prior to the interview to know what a person of your skills and experience can command in the marketplace. Be sure you have found out as much of the following information as you can.

The effect of your past salaries on your worth. If you received a high salary in the past, you can probably assume you are worth that much money, since others were willing to pay it to you. There is no reason to settle for less, unless the job is perfect in all other respects.

The salaries being paid to persons with similar job descriptions in the firm. While the information may be difficult to obtain, try to find out what a person who is doing the job you will be doing earns. Remember that there may be variations due to different degrees or experience, but you will at least have a starting point for negotiation.

There are two places you may find information on salaries within a particular company. Check back issues of the local newspapers, looking at the classified ads. When a company advertises a position, it often states offered salaries. While such salaries are only general, they will give you high and low guidelines.

You may want to look at past company newsletters. In-house newsletters are often available by writing to the public relations department of the firm, or by requesting them from the personnel department. Such newsletters may give information on recent raises or special benefits (such as stock distribution).

The salaries being paid to others in your field on a local/state/federal level. Know what the average salary of a person doing your job is. Of course, you will want to know the regional scale if it is higher, or the national scale if it is higher. This information is only for your benefit; it enables you to negotiate a salary intelligently and realistically.

There are two sources for information on salaries for those in the field. Industry or trade journals frequently publish surveys on salaries. The reference department of your local library will have a book entitled, *Index to Periodicals*. This book is a listing of magazines; reading through it will tell you what periodicals are available in your field.

Large employment agencies may have copies of salary surveys that they can release to you. Occasionally, they provide governmental publications that show the number of people within a particular industry, the average salary of a worker in that field, and the salary ranges.

The worth of your personal, special qualifications. In many instances, advanced degrees or extra schooling is worth a specific amount. Try to find out what that amount is and discuss it with the interviewer. Never underestimate your worth.

Salary Amount

While there are many other considerations that you will ponder when deciding whether to accept a job, the amount of salary you are to be paid will probably be of prime importance to you. Before you begin negotiating the actual dollar amount, ask yourself the following questions:

How often will my salary be raised? You may be willing to start at a low salary if you can be guaranteed that you will get raises at specified increments. If at all possible, get such increments in writing before you commit yourself to signing a contract.

Will I get an initial or a renewal bonus? Some firms give "incentive" money, lump sums that are given to you when you first join the firm as well as amounts that are given when you renew your contract. Ask the amounts of those sums and whether you are guaranteed to receive them.

Are there merit increases or bonuses? Often companies will give a semiannual merit review to determine the amount of your raise. Ask what factors are considered in such reviews and what the standard raise percentage or amount is. If there are bonuses for working overtime or bringing in a project under schedule, consider those as a part of your salary.

Is profit-sharing available? Especially in small companies that are just beginning, executives might be willing to share profits with the employees, especially in lieu of high salaries. If you feel confident that the firm will prosper, you might take a share of the profits and accept a lower salary.

Broaching the Topic

Money is difficult to discuss for most people. No one wants to appear grasping and avaricious, but everyone wants to know exactly how much money will be forthcoming. Before you begin the interview, determine whether or not to state your salary demands during the interview.

It is rarely good business to raise the question of your salary before the interviewer does. While you should have an idea in your mind of how much you want to be paid and the minimum amount you will accept, it is up to the interviewer to begin the negotiations on the subject. Allow him or her to make an offer. You then are free to make a counteroffer. If the interviewer asks you what salary you are looking for, be prepared to state a realistic salary range based on your research.

CHECKLIST

1. Am I willing to have my past salaries known?
2. Is it wise to "inflate" my salary?
3. Do I know what others in this firm doing my job are being paid?
4. Do I know my market worth on a regional or national level?
5. Do I know the worth of my special, personal qualifications (such as specific degrees or experience)?
6. May I find out how often I may get a raise and on what basis?
7. Is an initial or a renewal bonus available?
8. Are merit raises given and what factors are considered in their award?
9. Is profit-sharing available?
10. Am I prepared to let the interviewer broach the topic of salary?

After

YOU CANNOT ASSUME that your responsibilities are over when the interview is finished. Often, they are just beginning. Regardless of whether you are accepted or rejected by the firm, and regardless of whether you accept or reject the firm yourself, you must maintain a professional dignity in your future dealings with the company.

One thing you need to do right after the interview is send a letter to the person(s) you interviewed with, thanking them for their time (see the sample letter in Appendix A). The firm probably has interviewed many persons for the position you desire. While your goal is to be selected for that position, being rejected is not the end of the matter. You may find that the company is willing to consider you for other openings or for future projects. Many times firms recommend persons to other firms. Therefore, it is critical that your conduct after the interview be as competent and professional as your conduct during the interview.

This section tells you of the many variations possible, from the company's accepting you to your satisfaction, to the company's rejecting you to your dismay. It helps prepare you for any situation. Letters are included in Appendix A which you may use as samples for your own correspondence.

While this section is much shorter than the preceding ones, it is no less important. Simply because it is labeled *After* does not mean you do not need to read it before the interview. Take the time now to go through it carefully, to acquaint yourself with the many possible results of the interview.

DEALING WITH ACCEPTANCE OR REJECTION

1. UNQUALIFIED ACCEPTANCE OF NOTICE
2. COUNTEROFFER

3. REJECTION OF NOTICE
4. REQUEST FOR PARTICULARS

After the interview the company will probably contact you, usually by letter, to tell you whether you have been accepted or rejected. Regardless of which occurs, you want to handle the situation with professional dignity. The following outlines several different responses to the company's decision.

Unqualified Acceptance of Notice

In most cases, the applicant will accept the company's decision. If this is what you decide to do, be certain that you understand why such a decision was made. If you were offered the position, you should take the time to note what you did correctly, what impressed the interviewer and the firm. Such notes will be useful when you go through your next interview. If you were not offered the position, take note of what reasons the company offered. Often, such reasons will be vague and general, such as "Your qualifications, while impressive, do not exactly meet our current needs." However, if you have an idea of more specific reasons why you were rejected, take the time to analyze it for future reference.

Write a thank-you letter regarding the notice. Whether you were accepted or rejected, you still should write a short letter thanking the interviewer for his or her time and telling the company that you appreciated being considered. Such a letter, besides being simply courteous, will keep your name in the mind of the interviewer and the company. Should you want a favor or a position in the future, the good impression will be your first step towards obtaining one. Sample letters of thank-you for both an acceptance and a rejection are found in Appendix A.

Counteroffer

You may find that you have been given a qualified acceptance. Perhaps you were offered a different title or salary than you had hoped for. In this case, you might want to make a counteroffer, telling the firm that you would like to accept its offer if certain conditions were to be changed. A sample counteroffer letter is included in Appendix A. When writing such a letter, take into consideration the following.

Ask yourself whether you gave the impression during the interview that such a situation would be acceptable. If the interviewer felt that you wanted the position that he or she is offering to you now, making a counteroffer might be awkward. If there is any possibility of confusion, offer a rational reason for your counteroffer, such as changes in your family situation or your finances.

Make your counteroffer clear and detailed. Make certain that you state *specifically* what you want altered in the job offer. Give complete details as to what was offered (don't automatically assume that the person reading your letter remembers all the facts of the offer) and what you hope to receive.

Explain the reasons for your counteroffer. You will only bewilder the reader if you send a letter stating that you want changes made but giving no reasons for those changes. Remember when giving your reasons to put them in a frame of reference beneficial to the company. You will want to state that your talents would be better utilized by accepting the terms of your counteroffer, thus maximizing your contributions to the firm.

Be prepared to accept or reject the job proposal if the counteroffer is not accepted. If you make a counteroffer, you should be prepared to accept the job should your offer be approved. You should also know whether you would still accept the job should your offer be rejected, or whether you would refuse the position in such a situation. You should definitely have made up your mind on that subject *before* sending the counteroffer.

Make certain that the counteroffer is reasonable. You do not want to insult the firm and waste everyone's time with an offer that is impossible to accept. If the interviewer offered you a salary that you want doubled, you should not accept the job. Be sure that what you propose is logical and feasible.

Rejection of Notice

There may be a time when you decide to reject the decision that has been made. If you sincerely feel that an error has been made, either in analyzing your qualifications or in treating you with prejudice, you want to call that error to the attention of the proper person quickly and politely.

Try to understand why the decision was made. If the information in the rejection was not sufficient for you to understand why you were not accepted, try to obtain additional information before you become angry. Perhaps the letter you received was simply a time-saving form letter; ask for more particulars. If you do so courteously and not belligerently, most firms will be willing to give you that information. Such information could be considered constructive criticism that will help you prepare for your next interview.

If you feel that the decision was illegal or unfair because the rejection of you was based *solely* on race, age, or gender, or because of other unfair factors, you are free to take steps. There are many governmental agencies (listed in your telephone book) that will help you in your fight against a prejudiced employer. Remember, however, that most industries are small worlds. If you sue one business, you run the risk that all businesses will soon hear about it, to your possible detriment. Be very certain of your ground and be aware of the possible consequences before beginning any legal action.

Consider whether you want to try for the position again. Perhaps you were rejected solely due to a poor test score, or due to the lack of a specific qualification. You may want to ask to take the test again or ask to be reconsidered after you have received the proper training. Remember that the more detailed, polite, and enthusiastic your letter requesting a second try is, the more likely you are to obtain one.

Request for Particulars

One smart response to a rejection is to try to find out why you didn't get the job. Since you invested much time and effort preparing for the interview, you should attempt to gain as much as possible from it. Write the company, asking why you were rejected and whether the interviewer or firm has any suggestions that will help you in the future.

If you write such a letter, be certain that you are willing to accept the criticism. If the criticism is going to demolish your ego or make you belligerent and unwilling to accept it, then you are wasting your time asking to hear it. Be certain that you can accept the comments of others, even if they are extremely personal (for example, dealing with the way you dress or speak). You may not agree with the criticism, but you should recognize that it is an opinion you may have to deal with again.

Be willing to act upon the suggestions. In many instances, the chief reason for rejecting a candidate is his or her lack of qualifications or expertise. The person writing to you may recommend special courses or training classes that will be valuable to you. If you are willing to work and take such courses, then you were wise to ask for the criticism. If you have no intention of doing any more work, don't waste your time asking for the information.

Regardless of whether you are accepted joyfully, accepted grudgingly, or rejected, you must be able to accept the news and act upon it. You should always write to the firm with a brief "thank you"; in some situations you will want to ask questions or demand explanations of the rejection. The following checklist will help you with your response.

CHECKLIST

1. Do I understand the reasons the decision was made?
2. Am I willing to accept the job as it is offered?
3. Do I want to propose a reasonable, logical, and well-explained counteroffer?
4. Am I willing to accept the job, if my counteroffer is accepted?
5. Was my rejection illegal or unfair?
6. Am I willing to contest my decision, either within the firm or through legal action?
7. Do I want a second try at the position?

8. Do I want to learn exactly why I was rejected?
9. Am I willing to accept sincere criticism, no matter how personal, without being belligerent or hostile?
10. Am I willing to act upon the criticism to improve myself?

QUESTIONS YOU SHOULD ASK AFTER YOU HAVE BEEN OFFERED THE JOB

1. WORKING CONDITIONS
2. FINANCIAL CONSIDERATIONS
3. JOB SPECIFICS

Elsewhere in this book, you read of the important questions that should be asked during the initial interview to show the interviewer that you are interested and informed. This section suggests questions that you may want to ask *after* you have been offered the job. These questions cover matters concerned not so much with the duties of the position itself but with the conditions under which those duties must be performed.

Working Conditions

If you are going to be working within a building, you should be concerned with your surroundings. While financial and other considerations are important, the physical plant will affect you daily. These are a few topics you should ask about.

What will my office be like? While you do not want to present the negative, grasping image of someone who needs a carpeted office, plush furniture, and a window overlooking the park, you do want to know where you will be seated for eight hours a day. If you are not going to be given an office, you should know whether you will be in the middle of a large room with many others or be separated from your co-workers with a partition. You may find that among two or three job offers, you will take the one that gives you the nicest office.

What will security in the building and the parking lot be like? You want to have security in the parking lot so that your car is not stolen or vandalized. You also want to be able to feel secure in working in and walking to and from the building. If you work at night, ask about the lighting or the possibility of walking out in groups. If you work in a large city, you may want to know whether non-employees are prevented from wandering freely into the offices.

What parking will be available? If you drive to the office daily, you want to be certain that you will not start your day being frustrated because you are forced to fight for one of a few available parking spaces. While it is highly unlikely that you will be given a reserved or assigned space, you should ask to make certain that there are sufficient spaces.

Are there carpools arranged by the firm? Participating in a carpool that goes to or by your office can be a wonderful way to meet new people, feel more secure, save gasoline money, and have company on the drive.

Does the office permit smoking? Whether you are a smoker or a non-smoker, you will want to ask whether smoking is permitted in the office, not permitted at all, or restricted to a specific area. Be careful though not to make vehement, crusading statements either for or against smoking; you do not want to be labeled a troublemaker before you even begin the job.

Financial Considerations

SALARY AND OTHER COMPENSATION

Everyone is concerned with the monetary aspects of a job. Although financial considerations are discussed in more depth in the section entitled "Salary," the following questions should be noted as being important to discuss during an interview.

What will my salary be and how often will I receive it? Of course you will want to ask about your remuneration and the time in which it will be paid (weekly, biweekly, monthly). Be certain that you understand exactly what the lump sum breaks down into per day or per hour so that you can compare it with other job offers you may receive.

What bonuses may I receive? Get a complete list of any bonuses that are typical (such as at Christmas time) or that may be earned on merit (such as by finishing a project early). Find out whether you can get an individual bonus for a special effort, or whether you share a bonus with others in your division.

What is the average raise and the average time period between raises? You should have this information to be able to plan your personal finances. Of course, the interviewer will probably have to inform you that the raises are not definite; however, you will be able to get at least a general idea.

What dues, fees, or deductions are taken from my paycheck? Ask what unions, clubs, professional organizations, or other groups you are expected to join and who pays for the membership cost. Ask also whether your firm deducts any amounts from your check for any reason whatsoever (e.g., pension plan, enforced stock purchases).

Will I be paid for special education or training? You may find it necessary to take special advanced training in your subject. Companies might offer such training free, or they might reimburse you for your expenses if you can show that the courses were job-related. Occasionally, a firm will pay the expenses and also a special stipend to you for improving your knowledge.

Are moving or relocation expenses covered? If you must move, even across town, the expense can be very high. Many companies will pay all or part of this expense if you ask. Be certain, however, to get such a commitment in writing, including the date by which reimbursement will be made (usually you are required to pay the expenses out of your pocket; the company pays you back later).

"PERKS" AND BENEFITS

"Perks" are perquisites, little extra benefits that make the job nicer. For some people, an office is a perk; for others, the use of the company WATTS line is. Knowing the available perks may make the difference between your accepting this job or one with another firm.

What medical/dental plans are available? Having free or nearly free medical and dental care for you and your family could save you a great deal of money yearly. Be certain, however, to find out whether you may go to a physician of your choosing, or must go to the one supplied by the firm. Also find out what percentage of medical fees are covered, whether your dependents will be covered, and how much—if anything—you will have to pay in premiums or deductions. For some people, a good medical or dental plan can be worth thousands of dollars each year.

What life- or car-insurance plans are available? Again, you may be able to get a good group rate or a discount as a member of this particular firm. If you have a family, find out whether they will be covered as well.

Is there a credit union? Credit unions often give the lowest interest rates on loans, saving you thousands of dollars on a major purchase. They also are often easier to get a loan from in the first place. Occasionally, they offer free services such as checking and savings.

Do I get any store discounts? Especially with larger firms, you may find that your employee ID card entitles you to discounts at various stores. While such discounts are usually only 5–10%, they may add up to a large sum over the years.

Job Specifics

While you asked questions earlier regarding general job duties, there are probably many more specific questions you wish to ask at this point. The following questions are suggested.

Are transfers frequently given? This is actually a two-part question: Is the company likely to transfer me without my wanting to be re-located? May I get a transfer if I ask for one? You certainly want to know whether you will be forced to move yourself and your family should the company have an opening elsewhere. In the same manner, you want to know whether you could request a transfer to a more desirable branch or location.

Will I be given further education or training? Very few fields now allow you to remain active with a limited amount of knowledge. Most professions require periodic updating (this is especially true in such newer fields as computer science, or in such fluid fields as medicine). One consideration in your decision whether or not to take the job should be whether you will be given the opportunity to continue to expand your knowledge and add to your abilities.

Are there frequent compulsory meetings? If you are someone who dislikes meetings, this question will be important. You may find that meetings are held weekly, requiring you to give a progress report or work out deadlines and budgets.

What arrangements are available for sick days, overtime, and "comp" time? You should find out how many days a year you are allowed to take as sick days and what the policy is for allowing them. You should also try to find out what benefits you get from working overtime and how your "comp" time—that is, compensation time, or days you may take off for having worked on your regular day off or on a holiday—may be used.

CHECKLIST

1. What will my office be like?
2. What security will be available?
3. What will my take-home pay be?
4. May I receive further training or education?
5. Is advanced education or training offered free by the company?

6. Will the company reimburse me for additional outside education or training?
7. Who will pay for any moving and relocation costs?
8. Will I be required to pay expenses out of my pocket, to be reimbursed by the company later?
9. Does the firm pay all or part of the premiums for medical and dental plans?
10. If I require medical or dental services covered under an insurance policy, will I have to pay a set amount or a deductible?
11. What health and insurance plans are available?
12. What other perks will be available?
13. What is the company policy on transfers?
14. What is the policy on sick days/overtime/comp time?

Appendices

Sample Letters

• Letter Confirming Appointment Made Previously

George Marcy
1234 Miami Drive
Jessica, Maryland 20817
September 26, 198_

Ronald Frances
Personnel Director, Polyglot Computers
8839 East Jenn Avenue
Stras, California 92111

Dear Dr. Frances:

This letter is to confirm our appointment of October 10, 198_. Last month we arranged that I would meet with you in your office on that Tuesday at 10:00 a.m. to interview for the position of Senior Systems Analyst.

If a change must be made in these arrangements, please notify me as soon as possible. I may be reached at (619) 555–1212 or a letter may be sent to me at the above address.

I look forward to meeting with you. Thank you very much for your time and attention.

Sincerely,

George Marcy

• *Thank-you Letter for Interviewer's Time and Effort*

George Marcy
1234 Miami Drive
Jessica, Maryland 20817
October 11, 198_

Ronald Frances
Personnel Director, Polyglot Computers
8839 East Jenn Avenue
Stras, California 92111

Dear Dr. Frances:

Thank you very much for your time and attention during our recent interview. I enjoyed meeting with you and learning more about the opportunities available at Polyglot Computers.

If I may answer any further questions, or supply you with additional information, please do not hesitate to call me. I may be reached at (619) 555–1212 during business hours.

Again, thank you for your consideration. I appreciate the courtesy and patience with which you answered my questions and explained the responsibilities of the position. I look forward to hearing from you again soon.

Sincerely,

George Marcy

• *Follow-up Letter Restressing Qualifications and Interest*

George Marcy
1234 Miami Drive
Jessica, Maryland 20817
October 11, 198_

Ronald Frances
Personnel Director, Polyglot Computers
8839 East Jenn Avenue
Stras, California 92111

Dear Dr. Frances:

Thank you for your time and attention during our recent interview. While I was very interested in Polyglot Computers before our meeting, I am now more convinced than ever that I would enjoy working for and contributing to the firm.

My Bachelor's in Computer Science from California Polytechnic University at San Luis Obispo (a school noted for its computer science and engineering departments), and my Master's in Electrical Engineering from the same school give me a background that is, I think, very appropriate for the position of Senior Systems Analyst. My years of experience as a programmer, senior systems analyst, and instructor have taught me to be organized, logical, and efficient in finding and solving problems. These attributes, I feel, would be appreciated and well-utilized at Polyglot.

I was very impressed with the firm, the personnel, and the opportunities I saw. I would definitely like to be a part of the Polyglot team. If I can answer any further questions, or supply you with additional information, please do not hesitate to call me. I can be reached at (619) 555–1212 during business hours.

Again, thank you for your consideration. I appreciate the help you have already given me and look forward to hearing from you again soon.

Sincerely,

George Marcy

• *Letter Unconditionally Accepting the Position*

George Marcy
1234 Miami Drive
Jessica, Maryland 20817
October 28, 198_

Ronald Frances
Personnel Director, Polyglot Computers
8839 East Jenn Avenue
Stras, California 92111

Dear Dr. Frances:

I am very pleased to accept the position of Senior Systems Analyst with Polyglot Computers. I have carefully reviewed your letter of October 20, 198_, and find the terms discussed therein fair and mutually advantageous.

I will be beginning my new job on January 1, 198_, and am looking forward to a long and satisfactory career with Polyglot. I want to take this opportunity to thank you for the time and attention you gave me during and after our interview. Your help is appreciated.

If there are any materials I should receive for review prior to my beginning employment with Polyglot Computers, please send them to the address listed above. Again, thank you for your help.

Sincerely,

George Marcy

• *Letter Offering New/Alternate Conditions*

George Marcy
1234 Miami Drive
Jessica, Maryland 20817
October 28, 198_

Ronald Frances
Personnel Director, Polyglot Computers
8839 East Jenn Avenue
Stras, California 92111

Dear Dr. Frances:

Thank you for your letter of October 20, 198_, offering me the position of Senior Systems Analyst with Polyglot Computers. While I would like to accept your offer, as I am very interested in working for Polyglot, I am concerned about a few of the terms you suggest.

As we discussed during our interview, I feel that my experience and expertise would entitle me to a salary of $35,000 annually. I understand that your budgetary constraints make offering me such a salary difficult; therefore, I would like to suggest alternative financial considerations. I have in mind stock option plans and profit-sharing arrangements. Perhaps we could meet to discuss these arrangements in more detail.

Again, thank you for your offer. While I hesitate to accept the terms as given, I do feel that we will be able to negotiate mutually satisfactory terms with another personal meeting. Therefore, I look forward to hearing from you again soon. Thank you very much for your time and attention.

Sincerely,

George Marcy

• *Letter Rejecting Offer Without New Terms*

George Marcy
1234 Miami Drive
Jessica, Maryland 20817
October 28, 198_

Ronald Frances
Personnel Director, Polyglot Computers
8839 East Jenn Avenue
Stras, California 92111

Dear Dr. Frances:

Thank you very much for your letter of October 20, 198_, offering me the position of Senior Systems Analyst with Polyglot Computers. Although I would very much like to work with a firm as dedicated to growth and quality as Polyglot, I find that I am unable to accept your offer as stated.

As we discussed during our interview, I feel strongly that employees who have a direct financial interest in the profitability of a firm are better and more committed workers. I would like to obtain such an interest in any corporation for which I work. Therefore, I am going to continue looking for a position with a firm which will give me stock options and a profit-sharing plan.

Thank you for all your time and attention.

Sincerely,

George Marcy

• *Letter Rejecting Offer Completely*

George Marcy
1234 Miami Drive
Jessica, Maryland 20817
October 28, 198_

Ronald Frances
Personnel Director, Polyglot Computers
8839 East Jenn Avenue
Stras, California 92111

Dear Dr. Frances:

Thank you very much for your letter of October 20, 198_, offering me the position of Senior Systems Analyst with Polyglot Computers. Unfortunately, I am unable to accept your offer.

While the terms of your offer were generous, I have accepted a position with another firm. This position more fully meets my needs in such matters as salary and other financial incentives, responsibilities, and promotional opportunities.

I am grateful to you for the time and effort you took on my behalf. I wish you luck in finding a person who will be an asset to your firm as a Senior Systems Analyst. Again, thank you for all your help.

Sincerely,

George Marcy

• *Letter Questioning the Rejection*

George Marcy
1234 Miami Drive
Jessica, Maryland 20817
October 28, 198_

Ronald Frances
Personnel Director, Polyglot Computers
8839 East Jenn Avenue
Stras, California 92111

Dear Dr. Frances:

Thank you very much for your letter of October 20, 198_. While I am naturally disappointed that I was not chosen for employment as a Senior Systems Analyst with Polyglot Computers, I would like to thank you for the time and effort you took on my behalf.

I am still interested in being associated with a firm as dedicated to growth and quality as Polyglot. Therefore I would like to ask you for the particulars of my rejection. If you can point out any specific weaknesses in certain areas that I could deal with (by obtaining further education, for example) I would greatly appreciate your advice.

I hope that you will be able to take the time to give me this information. Please keep my resume and other material on file and consider me for future positions. Thank you for your attention. I look forward to hearing from you soon.

Sincerely,

George Marcy

• *Letter Requesting Future Consideration*

George Marcy
1234 Miami Drive
Jessica, Maryland 20817
October 28, 198_

Ronald Frances
Personnel Director, Polyglot Computers
8839 East Jenn Avenue
Stras, California 92111

Dear Dr. Frances:

Thank you for your letter of October 20, 198_. Naturally, I am disappointed that I was not given the job of Senior Systems Analyst, but I understand your reasons for not being able to offer me the position at this time.

My interview with you strengthened my positive impression of Polyglot Computers as an interesting, enjoyable place to work. I very much would like to be kept in consideration for future openings as they arise. I would appreciate your keeping my resume on file and notifying me should another opening occur for a person with my skills.

Thank you for your time and attention during our recent interview. I enjoyed meeting you and learning more about Polyglot. I appreciate the help you have given me and look forward to hearing from you again.

Sincerely,

George Marcy

Do's and Don'ts of Letter Writing

1. DO use quality, heavy bond paper (available at a stationery store or print/copy shop).

2. DO use a good typewriter with clear, clean print.

3. DO make certain your letter is sent to the right person. Use that person's name and title whenever possible.

4. DO maintain a professional, businesslike tone throughout.

5. DO make the point of the letter clear in the first paragraph.

6. DO thank the reader for his or her time and attention.

7. DO be concise. Respect the time of the person reading the letter.

8. DO be well-organized and coherent. *Plan* your letter before beginning to write.

9. DO have another person check your letter for grammatical errors. Be aware of commonly misused or misspelled words.

10. DO make certain you have included any extra documents referred to, such as a resume, newspaper clipping, or letter of reference.

1. DON'T use flimsy, erasable typing paper.

2. DON'T write the letter by hand or use a typewriter whose print comes out smeared or fuzzy.

3. DON'T send a letter to "To Whom It May Concern" or to an office in general.

4. DON'T try to be overly friendly, humorous, or witty.

5. DON'T write a vague, ambiguous letter that makes its recipient wonder what you wanted to say.

6. DON'T leave the impression you're doing the reader a favor by deigning to correspond with him or her.

7. DON'T think that a long letter is more impressive than a short one. Make your point; don't embellish or explain at length.

8. DON'T be repetitious, diffuse, or unclear. The reader should not have to read the letter twice to understand it.

9. DON'T assume that you can proofread your own writing. Another person can catch errors that you never noticed.

10. DON'T forget to include a self-addressed, stamped envelope if you want any documents returned.

Questions You Can and Can't Be Asked on an Interview

The following is a set of guidelines* for what you can and can't legally be asked prior to employment. Check with the Labor Department in your state or the Equal Employment Opportunities Commission for any updates or changes in these laws, or any variations in your area.

ACCEPTABLE	SUBJECT	UNACCEPTABLE
Name "Have you ever used another name?" /or/ "Is any additional information relative to change of name, use of an assumed name, or nickname necessary to enable a check on your work and education record? If yes, please explain."	**NAME**	Maiden name.
Place of residence.	**RESIDENCE**	"Do you own or rent your home?"
Statement that hire is subject to verification that applicant meets legal age requirements. "If hired can you show proof of age?" "Are you over eighteen years of age?" "If under eighteen, can you, after employment, submit a work permit?"	**AGE**	Age. Birthdate. Dates of attendance or completion of elementary or high school. Questions which tend to identify applicants over age 40.
"Can you, after employment, submit verification of your legal right to work in the United States?" /or/ Statement that such proof may be required after employment.	**BIRTHPLACE, CITIZENSHIP**	Birthplace of applicant, applicant's parents, spouse, or other relatives. "Are you a U.S. citizen?" /or/ Citizenship of applicant, applicant's parents, spouse, or other relatives.

*The Department of Fair Employment and Housing (California).

ACCEPTABLE	SUBJECT	UNACCEPTABLE
		Requirements that applicant produce naturalization, first papers, or alien card *prior to employment.*
Languages applicant reads, speaks, or writes.	**NATIONAL ORIGIN**	Questions as to nationality, lineage, ancestry, national origin, descent, or parentage of applicant, applicant's parents, or spouse. "What is your mother tongue?" /or/ Language commonly used by applicant. How applicant acquired ability to read, write, or speak a foreign language.
Questions regarding relevant skills acquired during applicant's U.S. military service.	**MILITARY SERVICE**	General questions regarding military services such as dates, and type of discharge. Questions regarding service in a foreign military.
	ECONOMIC STATUS	Questions regarding applicant's current or past assets, liabilities, or credit rating, including bankruptcy or garnishment.
"Please list job-related organizations, clubs, professional societies, or other associations to which you belong—you may omit those which indicate your race, religious creed, color, national origin, ancestry, sex, or age."	**ORGANIZA-TIONS ACTIVITIES**	"List all organizations, clubs, societies, and lodges to which you belong."
"By whom were you referred for a position here?" Names of persons willing to provide professional and/or	**REFERENCES**	Questions of applicant's former employers or acquaintances which elicit information specifying the applicant's race, color, religious creed, national

ACCEPTABLE	SUBJECT	UNACCEPTABLE
character references for applicant.		origin, ancestry, physical handicap, medical condition, marital status, age, or sex.
Name and address of person to be notified in case of accident or emergency.	**NOTICE IN CASE OF EMERGENCY**	Name and address of relative to be notified in case of accident or emergency.
Name and address of parent or guardian if applicant is a minor. Statement of company policy regarding work assignment of employees who are related.	**SEX, MARITAL STATUS, FAMILY**	Questions which indicate applicant's sex. Questions which indicate applicant's marital status. Number and/or ages of children or dependents. Provisions for child care. Questions regarding pregnancy, child bearing, or birth control. Name or address of relative, spouse, or children of adult applicant. "With whom do you reside?" /or/ "Do you live with your parents?"
	RACE, COLOR	Questions as to applicant's race or color. Questions regarding applicant's complexion or color of skin, eyes, hair.
Statement that photograph may be required after employment.	**PHYSICAL DESCRIPTION, PHOTOGRAPH**	Questions as to applicant's height and weight. Require applicant to affix a photograph to application. Request applicant, at his or her option, to submit a photograph. Require a photograph after interview but before employment.

ACCEPTABLE	SUBJECT	UNACCEPTABLE
Statement by employer that offer may be made contingent on applicant passing a job-related physical examination. "Do you have any physical condition or handicap which may limit your ability to perform the job applied for? If yes, what can be done to accommodate your limitation?"	**PHYSICAL CONDITION, HANDICAP**	Questions regarding applicant's general medical condition, state of health, or illnesses. Questions regarding receipt of Workers' Compensation. "Do you have any physical disabilities or handicaps?"
Statement by employer of regular days, hours, or shifts to be worked.	**RELIGION**	Questions regarding applicant's religion. Religious days observed /or/ "Does your religion prevent you from working weekends or holidays?"
"Have you ever been convicted of a felony, or, within (specified time period) a misdemeanor which resulted in imprisonment?" (Such a question must be accompanied by a statement that a conviction will not necessarily disqualify applicant from the job applied for.)	**ARREST, CRIMINAL RECORD**	Arrest record /or/ "Have you ever been arrested?"
Statement that bonding is a condition of hire.	**BONDING**	Questions regarding refusal or cancellation of bonding.